Contents

Introduction

It has been stated that nothing new has been said on the subject of leadership for well over 2000 years. This, of course, is a deliberately provocative statement but as the Chinese philosopher, Lâo Tse, who wrote on the subject circa 500 BC is often quoted in articles and books on leadership, then maybe there is a thread of truth in the thought.

If, however, nothing new has been said on the subject for all this time, why is it is a matter of such interest and debate? Why do people refer to it as such a challenging concept and, most of all, why put down more words on it?

The reality is that leadership has been defined and redefined many times over the centuries and perhaps never more so than in the last few years. However, something elusive still remains about the concept. Like poetry or religion, it often defies logical analysis while at the same time retaining a logic of its own. Consequently, many studies, by attempting to subject it to scientific scrutiny or cold reason, often miss the mark and leave the reader unsatisfied.

The reason for this is that leadership, whether in a political, military, or commercial setting, is about emotion. People react to leaders and their approaches in emotional ways. Thus, a totally factual or systematic approach to the subject is likely to miss the mark as it will not cover the whole spectrum of insights, emotions, and activities that make for effective leadership. It is a knowledge of these intangibles, however, that can enable an ordinary person to become an effective leader.

In writing this book, my approach has been to try to use both a logical as well as a more intuitive approach to the subject using largely examples from the world of work but occasionally those from other theatres of leadership. In doing so I hope to cover the subject more fully and to add a new dimension for the reader, whichever approach is favoured.

In scoping the subject, a number of definitions of leadership will be examined and compared. Before doing so, I would like to give my own.

Being a leader is something you *do* rather than something you are. It is the ability to bring out a number of talents and to operate effectively through other people, making them gladly accept your goals while still having the freedom to do things their way. A good leader therefore understands and meets people's positive expectations of how they wish to be led.

Becoming a good leader is something you *choose* to do through a process of action and self-discovery.

To say that leadership is important in all walks of life is a major understatement. It is crucial. It is only through it that work, society, and even the world can be changed for the better. For most of us, the most direct experiences both of leading and of being led stem from the world of work. We have bosses and often have people who report to us. The behaviour that is of central concern to this book is the way that we behave towards each other at work, so perhaps it is there that we should start our voyage of discovery into the subject.

However, this voyage is also into yourself. If you broadly accept the definition of leadership contained here then you will see that the process of becoming a leader is largely up to you; it is also about you and involves finding what may, at present, be hidden.

Acknowledgement

I would like to thank my colleagues for their help and advice. I would especially like to thank the many 'students' who have attended leadership programmes at Sundridge Park—from whom I have learnt so much!

What is this thing called leadership?

Leadership is all about people. That is one reason why it can be hard to define; it is certainly the reason why the subject has exercised a strange fascination over the years.

As opposed to management, which is about method and procedure, leadership is about *you* as a person and about the people with whom you work. The quality of the leader affects individuals, teams, organizations, and nations. It is one of the most important factors in humanity but we know so little about it. Perhaps the best place to start is by looking at people as leaders, at work.

Forgetting the words 'leader' or 'leadership' think back to people you have known in your working life to date. Specifically, think about the best and worst bosses you have ever worked for. What was it about them both as individuals and in *what they did*, i.e. their behaviour, that made them either so good or so bad?

It is quite probable in describing the worst boss you have ever worked for that you will come up with words along the following lines.

- A bully who always looked to blame others.

- Would always pass the buck, if at all possible.

- Had no opinion on anything and was totally indecisive!

- I hated working for a politician who took all the credit.

- I wasn't kept informed and I felt powerless.

- A rotten delegator making me become totally frustrated.

- Never listened and saw me only as a cog in the machine.

- My boss didn't understand my job!

These words describe either despots or incompetents. They do not describe leadership behaviour. So, moving on to the words that you may have used to describe the best boss, it is probable that they will incorporate many of the following thoughts and emotions:

- My boss delegated, and was demanding, but supported me when it got tough.

- If I did well I was given credit where it was due.

- Went out of the way to develop others in their jobs.

- Was actually interested, and listened to me.

- Could be tough when necessary, but was also consistent and decisive.

- It was a real pleasure to work for someone who was flexible and creative.

- Showed passion and courage and I therefore felt glad to follow.

There are a number of steps between listing desirable behaviours and either obtaining a clear-cut definition of leadership or pointing the way to how the busy and beleaguered manager can adopt them. However, it is often with single sentences rather than long and elaborate descriptions that we can best pinpoint a subject—especially an elusive one. A variation on this approach was successfully used by Management Centre Europe in 1988. The centre wished to define further the personal qualities that good leaders brought to their roles and asked over 1000 European managers to state what they considered to be the attributes of a successful business leader and then, whether their own chief executive had those qualities. The results are interesting and are displayed in Fig 1.1.

What they show is that there was a high level of agreement among the respondents as to what they desired from their leaders and at the same time general agreement that they were not on the receiving end of these desirable behaviours or, and this is probably far worse, often on the receiving end of less desirable behaviours.

Leadership brainstormed

The words and phrases in the findings of Figure 1.1 go a long way to describing what is desirable or not, as the case may be, in leaders in most walks of life. Perhaps the pieces of the jigsaw are now beginning to come together, however, and before finally attempting to define this elusive concept let us look at one more attempt to hang meaningful words around it.

	What they should have %	What my present CEO has %
Able to build effective teams	96	50
Knows how to listen	93	44
Capable of making decisions on their own	87	66
Know how to retain good people	86	39
Surrounds themselves with the top people	85	50
Energetic	75	62
Innovative	83	47
Visionary	79	45
Have high ethical standards	76	53
A strong presence	74	51
Strong willed	70	65
Mature	67	57
Knows how to manage committees	65	45
International in outlook	64	59
Understands new technologies	64	47
A good presenter	62	47
Ambitious	62	65
Physically fit	60	51
Charismatic	54	34
Democratic	40	31
Literate	38	41
Motivated by power	35	59
Look like leaders	30	44
Compassionate	30	24
Numerate	29	37
Are industry figures	26	38
Admired by employees at all levels	20	29
Motivated by money	17	40
Are public figures	14	22
Ruthless	10	28
Paternalistic	6	24

Figure 1.1 Differences between perception and reality.

A group of people with a keen interest in the subject met at Sundridge Park in order to brainstorm and debate the subject. The group consisted of consultants, practising managers and academics, both Europe and the USA were represented. The words 'Leadership is...' were written up on a flipchart and then battle commenced.

By the end of the first bout of the brainstorm a long list of words, expressions, guesses, and 'gut feelings' faced the group. Not everybody there agreed with everything that had been said, but in the true spirit of the brainstorm, had refrained from expressing their disagreement. What was agreed was that the list was nothing if not comprehensive and that any one individual who managed to satisfy all these criteria would be pretty extraordinary. The list was then drastically shortened although the brainstormers felt that if the following ideas were omitted, the description of leadership would be lacking. What remained were the following thoughts.

Leadership is:

- Managing change and moving groups to new targets.
  —Getting exceptional results through others.
  —Managing and knowing yourself.
  —Working with and through teams.
  —Having a vision and being able to develop strategies from it.

- Respecting other people but being demanding of them.
  —Being open to ideas and listening.
  —Knowing how to inspire others yet also how to empower them to complete the task.
  —Communicating effectively and persuasively!

The complex range of talents encapsulated in these few sentences will be the essence of this book.

Leaders named

The group then decided to name as many leaders as possible in the space of five minutes; the only restrictions were that the leaders mentioned should be well known and that their leadership should have made an impact. The list, when completed, was fairly predictable although there were some surprises in it.

The leaders were:

Florence Nightingale	Geronimo
Martin Luther King	Benito Mussolini
Nelson Mandela	John F. Kennedy
Abraham Lincoln	Napoleon
Winston Churchill	Charles de Gaulle
Emmeline Pankhurst	Jesus Christ
'Just William' Brown	M. Gandhi
Adolph Hitler	T. E. Lawrence

Mao Tse Tung	Nelson
Lord Hanson	Ho Chi Minh
Theodore Roosevelt	Golda Meir
Mother Teresa	Apostle Paul
Richard Branson	Michael Edwards
Anita Roddick	

The brainstormers agreed that while not all the names could by any means be called 'good' leaders, either they were in roles that forced them to indulge in certain activities that could be called leadership activities or they chose to act in certain ways that made others follow them. The challenge was then to try to agree on whether there was anything that they all had in common.

The common factors of leadership

The group found it impossible to reach a consensus on characteristics that applied to them all, but the following thoughts summarize those attributes that were considered to be common to the majority. What particularly struck the group about them was that:

- They were principled, often set out to change things, and were challenging.

- They had great drive, were sometimes intense but always courageous.

- Their followers noticed that a relationship was being cultivated with them.

- They had ideas that motivated and inspired others by giving meaning to the situation. This meaning made future benefits worth working for.

- Many had early experience of leading and became committed and focused early in their lives.

- They were consistent and durable but at the same time could be ruthless and politically astute.

Another major factor about all these people was that they were *noticeable*. However, it was what they *did* that made them noticeable.

(At this stage William Brown was disqualified since he was a fictional character, although some members of the group felt that he met more of the criteria than many of the others on the list!)

Is it not possible, however, to pull all of these thoughts together into some simple, easily understandable definition that encapsulates the whole subject neatly? The answer is that it is of course possible, but that the subject can be elusive. Thus, for it to be fully grasped, it must be approached in more than one way in order to give it true meaning.

Other definitions

In the introduction I gave my definition of leadership. Here now are some other definitions. After they have been made, the rest of this book will concentrate on enlarging on them, relating them to the key thoughts that were listed earlier and, above all, trying to illustrate what is in them for *you*. It will concentrate on how the thoughts on leadership can make you more effective, more confident, and more content as a leader both within and outside a working environment.

An all-embracing definition of leadership goes as follows:

'It is that part of a manager's activities by which he or she influences the behaviour of individuals or groups towards a desired result. Success depends upon the human relations skills and personality of the manager to meet the intrinsic and extrinsic needs of the group being led.'

In many respects this definition says it all. However, it says it in such general terms as to make it of questionable use. More significantly, it says it in such a passionless way as to miss the true spirit of the word. Leadership is about emotion, people react to leaders in emotional and not always logical ways. Consequently, the following definition from an address by Field Marshal Lord Slim, when Governor-General of Australia, may be closer to the mark, especially as the first definition does nothing to clear up the old confusion between leadership and management.

'There is a difference between leadership and management. Leadership is of the spirit, compounded of personality and vision; its practice is an art. Management is of the mind, a matter of accurate calculation . . . its practice is a science. Managers are necessary; leaders are essential.'

Leaders—born or made?

Slim's is a far more satisfactory statement and the final sentence is unquestionably true. It is often taken as the classic definition of leadership but does fail in one major way. There is an underlying assumption in it that leaders are born that way, and that if you have not exhibited clear signs of leadership ability by an early age you might as well give up. Adoption of this line of thinking must in the past have stifled many a potential leader who was just waiting for circumstance or opportunity to test out his or her abilities.

Indeed, there has been a wealth of muddled thinking on the subject of whether the ability to lead is born into some individuals and will show itself, in the same way that some people are born with good singing voices and others are not, or whether the ability to lead is something that can be developed in people. A rather nice illustration of this muddled approach can be found in the report on a young officer in the British army that stated, 'Jones is not a born leader . . . yet.'

What may well be coming through by now is that many attempts to define the concept have been problematical, especially when one tries to distinguish it from the concept of management. This is a difficulty that has been articulated time and time again by those holding down management jobs of any description.

The difference between leadership and management

John Kotter made perhaps one of the most detailed and helpful distinctions between leadership and management and in so doing further described both. Let us briefly examine his definitions and then regard the question as having been answered, for the time being, at least.

Management, he said, involved the following and it can be seen that this is predominantly activity based:

- *Planning and budgeting*   This involves target-setting. Establishing procedures for reaching target. Allocating the resources necessary to meet the plans.

- *Organizing and staffing*   This means setting the organization structure. Hiring the right people and establishing incentives.

- *Controlling and problem-solving*   Again this means the monitoring of results against the plan. Identifying problems and working out how to solve them.

Everything here is concerned with logic, structure, analysis, and control and as Kotter says, if done well, it produces predictable results on time.

Leadership, on the other hand, requires a different set of actions and indeed a completely different mind-set:

- *Creating a sense of direction*   This is usually born out of dissatisfaction with the status quo. It is challenged. Out of this challenge a vision for something different is born.

- *Communicating the Vision*   The vision must meet the realized or unconscious needs of other people and the leader must work to give it credibility. On the basis that all change requires a critical mass of support the leader must create a culture within the organization that backs it.

- To do this the leader must: *energize, inspire*, and *motivate*   These three words encapsulate much of what a leader must be seen to do, people must be kept moving, enthusiasm must be bred and maintained and when the going is tough they must be supported and helped.

All of these activities involve dealing with people rather than things. As people are unpredictable and often bloody-minded, they call for a large investment of *self* from the leader. If it is done well, with passion and commitment, then it will produce impetus for change. It could well be said that where no change is desired, management will suffice. Where change is needed management alone will be found to be lacking and the need for leadership will come to the fore.

A concept that has emerged in both the Kotter and the Slim definitions is that of the leader's 'vision'. Nowadays this word is ubiquitous and like many fashionable expressions its true meaning can be lost. Without doubt, leaders must have a vision of what they wish to achieve, but the word is very emotive and can have supernatural connotations. This will be explored in depth in Chapter 3 but for the time being the following definition is both amusing and apt:

A vision is having a picture of the cathedral in mind when you and your people first start to mix the concrete.

Looking at your job

At this stage a useful exercise for the leader in a management job is to look at the job and to break it down into those parts that are true leadership and those parts that are something else. Most jobs of a certain seniority are likely to have an element of leadership. They will also contain a large element of management; now it might be useful to adopt the word 'administration' as a more apt description of what goes on in this part of the individual's work. As most people, even the very senior, report to someone else, the job will have 'followership' contained in it. Finally, it will contain elements of technical knowledge, as nobody in authority can afford to be ignorant of those special factors that drive the business.

One way of looking at your job in this way is to draw a picture of it. Figure 1.2 shows a job divided up like a cake, the different slices portraying the amount of time in the job that is dedicated to the different elements. What you can then do is redraw your job to illustrate the amount of time and effort that you consider *should* be dedicated to the different elements. If the gaps are large, then it is worth questioning whether you are being truly effective and whether you are spending enough time on leadership activities. Is management the easier option?

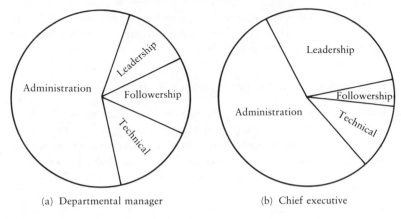

(a) Departmental manager   (b) Chief executive

Figure 1.2 Breakdown of roles within job.

Figure 1.2 also illustrates the different proportions of various jobs of dissimilar seniority that might be dedicated to the different elements. Even the CEO has a followership role and no CEO can afford to lose contact completely with the product or technology of the business.

The leader's choices

If job holders are able to look at their jobs and make decisions concerning the amount of time that will be dedicated to leading, following administration, or the technical side, then any individual has equal freedom of choice to decide *how* to lead. The question of 'how' can be dealt with in terms of 'where' the leader leads from and then in terms of the 'style' of leadership that the individual adopts.

In both cases it boils down to a matter of choice! You can choose the style and approach that you use and adapt it to meet the needs of the situation in which you find yourself. The tragedy for so many, both leaders and those they lead, is that they do not realize that they have a choice regarding the styles or behaviours that they use; if they did realize this fact then maybe life for many would be easier and the role of leader less stressful.

The question of *where* the leader leads from is an interesting one and one that encapsulates many of the dangerous preconceptions of leadership. The traditional and most common image of a leader is probably of a male, military figure leading and urging his troops into battle. It is an upfront role and the whole outcome of the proceedings depends on the courage and inspiration of the leader. Many think that this is the only way to lead. It is not. It is one way and at times an excellent way but we cannot all charge ahead yelling 'Once more unto the breach, dear friends'. For some of us this would be acting completely out of character and for many occasions, especially given the complexity of today's scenarios, this sort of approach would be totally out of place.

LEADING FROM THE FRONT—EL CID STYLE

In the epic film about the liberation of Spain from Moorish invaders, El Cid, a minor nobleman, manages to unite a disorganized and downhearted Spanish people behind him to take on and defeat a stronger foe. As the story unfolds, El Cid, stoically played by Charlton Heston, prepares for the final sequence of battles that will enable him to at last achieve his aims. The penultimate battle is fought against a spectacular background of sea and castles and in it the unthinkable happens: El Cid is wounded!

He staggers back to the safety of the city he is defending with an arrow in his chest. In pain and frustration he calls the surgeons to him. The surgeons examine him and then report back. 'It is a serious wound, the arrow must be removed,' they declare.

El Cid looks worried. 'What will be the results of your removing the arrow?' he asks. They inform him that there will be a considerable loss of blood and that he will be too weak to fight in battle for a long time. 'But I must lead my people against the enemy in the morning', he gasps. 'They will not succeed without me!'

'If we remove the arrow, you will be too weak to lead your army,' reply the surgeons. There is a pause. 'What will happen if you leave the arrow in me?' El Cid eventually asks. 'Then you will die of internal bleeding, tonight,' he is informed.

'But I have to lead my people tomorrow,' he states dramatically. 'Leave the arrow in place!' In summary, he elects to die and the audience are left to wonder why, until the final scenes of the film, when the dead body of El Cid is bolted into his armour and strapped onto his horse. His army, thinking that he is still alive, cheer and then follow his corpse as the horse charges towards the enemy. Needless to say the enemy are routed and, as the film ends, the camera pans towards our hero on his horse as it gallops into the sunset, carrying him into history.

Unfortunately, El Cid never realized that there were other ways to lead or other positions from which to do so. If he had, he might well have had the satisfaction of seeing his life's work completed and of enjoying the fruits of his leadership.

If the El Cid example seems unrealistic then consider a plaintive cry made by many managers when asked to be less up front and to allow their followers to do more: 'But nobody does it better.' Another position from which he could have chosen to lead might have been the middle.

Leading from the middle

Those who opt to lead from the middle have realized that they cannot be everywhere at once, even if that were desirable. There will be followers, or subordinates, who have talents and who want to be given a chance to contribute and to prove their worth. What they need is someone who will be there to pass on information, give advice and directions when they are needed, and who will help coordinate their efforts with the work of other people. They are not looking for someone to make all the decisions for them, to lead every negotiation or to be involved in solving every problem that arises. What they do want, however, is to have someone to consult and from whom to receive both information and advice.

THE DIVISIONAL MANAGER

At a division of Plessey Electronic Systems the general manager decided to set up a business control centre. He asked the six divisional managers who reported to him to move out of their departments and to move into a row of offices in a completely separate building. The general manager established himself in another separate location but stated that at least he could call together his six main 'reports' when he needed to.

Quite soon things began to go wrong. Mistakes were made at a departmental level and people complained about lack of communication and the remoteness of management. The divisional managers on the other hand felt overmanaged. Finally, one of them broke away. Frustrated by his remoteness from his department but not fully sure whether it was the separate location that was causing all the problems, he moved back into his department. Owing to the reorganization there was no separate office for him to use so, to make a point, he had his desk placed in the middle of the open plan office.

Soon, the volume and quality of his department's work began to improve. The divisional manager had, while away from his department, been forced into a less interventionist approach. He was there but he now let people come to him. As a result his time was spent in helping people where necessary and in both giving and receiving information. He was still in touch with events but his staff felt freer, more confident, and were likely to make good decisions.

By both mentally and physically rebelling against the attempt to make him the epitome of the upfront leader, the divisional manager had found that managing from the middle was more effective for his situation and that it demanded a different set of skills.

Leading from the rear

The third position from which to lead is the rear. But how can this be?

Perhaps the easiest way to describe this way of leading is by the use of another example. In 1992, British newspapers printed the obituary of a Colonel Maurice Buckmaster. The vast majority of readers had never heard of him but those that did bother to read the obituaries would have then wondered why his name was not well known, as here was someone who had debatably done more to shorten the Second World War than many generals and certainly most politicians. So, why is the name so little known?

THE SPYMASTER

Maurice Buckmaster, a young army officer, joined a newly formed organization called Special Operations Executive (SOE) in 1941. As he spoke fluent French and had a good knowledge of France, he was asked to head up SOE's French section.

SOE was part of the British secret service effort and Buckmaster became, in effect, the 'spymaster'. The objectives of SOE were to plant agents in occupied Europe and France in order to foster the spirit of resistance, work with the French Resistance or the Maquis, and generally to contribute to Churchill's stated ambition to 'set Europe ablaze'. During his time as head of French section, Buckmaster recruited, trained, briefed, and motivated no less than 370 men and 39 women agents to work in occupied territory. The chances of capture were high. Of those who were sent, 91 men and 13 women never came back, and those who were captured could expect torture and a miserable death.

Among the brave people he recruited were Yeo-Thomas (code name The White Rabbit), Peter Churchill, Richard 'Xavier' Heslop, Odette Churchill, and Violet Szabo. Yeo-Thomas, 'Odette', and Szabo ended up in concentration camps after capture. Szabo died.

But Buckmaster, who was affectionately known as 'Buck' by his agents, was never allowed to parachute in himself. His job was to motivate and to send people to carry out difficult work requiring great courage. Once they had arrived in France his only connection with them was through 'illicit' radio contact or through coded messages broadcast across Europe by the BBC.

Buckmaster made things happen through other people, but without his initial work they would have had neither the will nor the ability to succeed. An example of leadership from the rear, and because of that he never received the recognition he deserved.

Many a sales manager might be unconsciously working on the same model of behaviour as Maurice Buckmaster. It can be and often *is* successful.

Models of leadership

So the leader has choices and the way that these choices are exercised will play a large part in determining the degree of success. Throughout much of the current thinking on the subject runs the thread of choosing the correct method or style of leadership in order to be as effective as possible in coping with a given situation.

It is not the intention here to plough exhaustively through the many theories that exist on the subject, suffice it to say that the choice of the most effective style has exercised the ingenuity of many worthy academics over the last few decades. Grids have been drawn to illustrate varying leadership styles ranging from the laid back 'country club' manager to the more intense individual who insists on efficiency in operations as a priority over human considerations. Another approach which I personally find more illuminating is the decision-making continuum of Tannenbaum and Smith.

A decision-making continuum

This continuum takes as its premise the concept that managers or leaders can choose how much authority to exert over a situation and therefore how much or how little authority to give to their subordinates. For example, at one end of the continuum the leader allows the followers almost complete freedom to organize and carry out the task in their own way, exercising only minimal supervision. Another leader may prefer to work with the team and to solve the problems jointly with its members, while another may prefer to do all the decision-making alone but will at least bother to try and convince the team that it is the right solution, in other words 'sell' them the idea. Finally, at the opposite end of the continuum to the democratic leader is the one who simply announces that a decision has been made. The implication here is: 'Like it or else!'

The main stages on the continuum can be broadly broken down into:

- Delegating

- Participating

- Selling and

- Telling

Once again the key message here is that there is no one right or wrong way to operate. Being right depends on choosing the correct or most appropriate style for the situation at hand.

Exercising your choices—situational leadership

Take, for example, the case of the captain of an ocean liner. This captain is the most relaxed and democratic sailor ever to sail the seven seas. The captain has total confidence in the ship's officers and allows them to make important decisions concerning the running of the ship. This is fine until the ship, which just happens to be called the *Titanic*, loses an encounter with an iceberg and starts to do a nosedive towards the bottom of the Atlantic. At that stage only one approach is appropriate. The captain must act in an authoritative and forceful manner. He must demand complete obedience and swift action on his instructions. Delegating, participating, and selling are definitely out. The only way in which complete disaster can be avoided is through the exercise of an authoritative 'Telling' style of leadership.

With the idea that the choice of the right type of behaviour to match the situation was the key to success came the development of a popular method of looking at leadership behaviour called 'situational leadership'. This was devised by Hersey and Blanchard and then further developed by Professor Blanchard. As it is an excellent shorthand to describe the choices of leadership behaviour open to us, it is worth looking at in more detail.

The choice of correct leadership behaviour is seen to be dependent on three factors:

1. the leader

2. the followers

3. the situation

Characteristics of the leader

How is the leader used to leading? What is the leader's perception of the followers? Do they appear competent? Does the leader inately trust other human beings to take the initiative and work hard or does the leader believe that most people will avoid work and shirk responsibility if they can? All of these factors will influence how the leader elects to lead. However, as they are mainly ego-centred rather than other-centred, they will not necessarily mean that the correct approach for the situation is chosen.

The leader may come closer to getting it right by looking at the followers' characteristics.

Characteristics of the followers

What style of leadership are the followers used to? A drastic change in approach by a new leader may well confuse them, especially if it is a move from telling to delegating. What is the followers' estimation of their own competence? How confident are they? How much uncertainty or ambiguity are they able to tolerate?

An examination of these and other factors must govern the leader's choice of leadership style towards these particular subordinates. And then, of course, there is the situation itself.

Characteristics of the situation

This is a major determinant. How urgent is it? Is the work new or routine? Do mistakes matter?

During a training programme, I once argued that a good leader had to allow subordinates to make mistakes as this enabled them to learn. I was successfully challenged by a senior civil servant who told me that her job was to lead a team that prepared answers to anticipated Parliamentary questions during prime minister's question time. Wrong answers were simply not permitted by Mrs Thatcher and so in the civil servant's case there were very real limits to whether she could take a delegating approach. She had to double-check everything!

Situational-based leadership styles

Based on an understanding of these three elements, Hersey and Blanchard identified four different leadership styles that the leader could choose to use.

Style 1 A directive approach

This is characterized by lots of direction for subordinates but little support. They are expected to act fast and not to question orders. Key words here could be: 'When I say jump, I mean jump!'

This style is often used for short time-scales or where the staff are new to the job. Alternatively, the work itself may be of a simple nature.

Style 2 A coaching approach

Here the leader adopts a style that is both directive and supportive. The approach will be on the following lines: 'Here is a task and this is the way I want you to do it. If on the other hand you run into difficulties or need any help, do come and see me. My door is always open, etc.'

This approach is often effective when dealing with people who have some job knowledge but who are still inexperienced enough to need help and coaching.

A NEED FOR A COACHING APPROACH

Reflection on work with trainee chartered accountants showed that it was after a few weeks or months of training that they most needed this approach. When they first started their training contracts they were full of enthusiasm and were keen to be told how to make a start. However, when they had been on their first audit (and found out how staggeringly boring the work could be), and embarked on the long course of study for their professional examinations (and started to realize how difficult they were), then that was the time that they needed most support as well as direction from a coaching-orientated boss.

Style 3 A supporting approach

This style is most often appropriate when managers of some seniority are working together. Here the approach of the senior individual is on the following lines: 'Look, you have experience and I trust you to do a good job. You know what to do and I don't need to spell it out for you. On the other hand, if you have any problems, come and see me. I will help you. We can work it out together'. So the approach is undirective but supportive.

Style 4 A delegating approach

A style that is less often used. It presupposes that the subordinate has reached a high level of competence in the job and that the leader has considerable trust in that person. Here the leader's approach might well be: 'Look, you are a senior and experienced member of staff. You know the job and you don't need me to tell you what to do. Do it your own way and don't come to me for help all the time. You are paid to take responsibility and make decisions. So do so!'

Uses of the model

This situational leadership model complements the framework of telling, selling, participating, and delegating. As already mentioned, it illustrates the choices of behaviour open to the leader and the essentials that must be borne in mind when making the choices. Applying it is a good first step on the road to being an effective leader but it is only a first step. The role of leader is too complex, and too much a mixture of the emotional and the illogical for it to be totally packagable in one neat model.

Let the model serve, however, as a means of illustrating the choice of behaviours open to a leader. But it is now necessary to examine some vital things that the leader cannot afford to forget and then broaden the argument out to investigate what it can mean to you.

SO, WHAT'S IN IT FOR YOU? THE STRENGTH THAT CHOICE GIVES

'Out of the strong came forth sweetness': this, you may recall, was the riddle that Samson posed to the Philistines. He never expected them to guess the answer as the riddle was nothing if not obscure. However, less obscure might be another saying: 'Out of the sweetness of choice comes forth strength'. Leaders must appreciate that the models described above give them the strength of choosing a variety of behaviours. There are, on the other hand, several other aspects about being a leader that should not be forgotten and they are not so much about choice of behaviour as about forgetting some key concepts at your peril. An examination of these key concepts will form the final part of our definition of leadership. The remaining chapters will be devoted to explaining them in the context of your own self-discovery and development as a leader.

Fundamentals

The first fundamental that the leader cannot afford to ignore is that of the demands of the *task*, the *team*, and the *individual*. John Adair in *Effective Leadership* developed the thesis that the good leader must take into account and balance these three demands. Ignore just one factor and the validity of the leader's position is at risk.

The task is what the leader sets out to do or achieve. It is in effect the leader's *raison d'être* and to forget it is to dissolve into aimless wandering which will soon sabotage credibility.

The team is the group of people with whom the leader must work to achieve the task. The group will have its own needs. Needs perhaps to develop and feel valued as a group, or needs to be heard or to be given resources.

Finally, the team is made up of individuals. They too have needs. Needs to be heard, special concerns, and anxieties. Needs, perhaps to be valued by the leader for their own personal contribution.

The needs of task, team, and individual exist as interdependent entities. The credibility of the leader depends on the three different needs being met and balanced. Perhaps one of the clearest examples of a leader balancing these needs can be seen in Field Marshal Montgomery.

MONTGOMERY, A LEADER WHO MET THE NEEDS

'Monty' arrived to take over the command of the British 8th Army in 1942. It was at a time when the British were being systematically beaten by the brilliant soldiering of Rommel. The 8th Army was in disarray and morale was at rock bottom. Right from the start Monty emphasized that he and his men had but one purpose in life and that was to beat Rommel—to win. He stressed this time and time again and added that any soldier or officer who did not share this aim had no place with him—he would help them on their way back to Britain. Perhaps he had read Shakespeare's *Henry V*.

At the same time he looked at the army itself. He noted its low morale and its lack of resources and then pushed Churchill again and again to send him more weapons, more armour, more resources—even at the expense of the war effort elsewhere. Suddenly the army realized that it had a commander that really cared about it and that perhaps, after all, they did have a chance of winning.

And then, of course, Monty took an interest in the soldiers who made up the army. He took time to speak to them, he heard their complaints, he listened to their point of view. For every private soldier to whom he spoke, the word went round to dozens of others—that the boss was human and that he cared.

Shortly, Monty wrought a massive transformation in the army and the victory at El Alamein was debatably the turning point of the Second World War. A combination of task, team, and individual had prevailed, and remembering these essentials remains one of the keys to successful leadership.

Other essentials

So what else must the aspiring leader remember? At this stage it is worth reminding ourselves of a few other essentials. First, management is about logic, leadership about touching people's emotions. The totally logical leader will not touch people's hearts and will therefore probably fail, so what does that mean to the leader? It means that the leader must have a vision or compelling dream of what can or should be achieved. Lose the dream and the message becomes passionless. Lose the passion and people drift away from you.

People will also drift away from the leader who has a compelling vision that does not relate to the wants and needs of the followers. Leaders *always* deal with people and people have WIFMs. What are WIFMs? Very simple, WIFM stands for 'what's in it for me?'

Forget that people have WIFMs and the passion of your vision becomes as 'sound and fury, signifying nothing'! WIFMs will be revisited in detail in Chapter 5. They are crucial!

An inevitable decline?

Finally, a chilling note on which to end a chapter. Is there an inevitable process of *birth*, *growth*, *maturation* and *decline* of leadership in an individual?

A great deal of evidence appears to support this concept. Although some people have 'greatness thrust upon them' usually in the form of a significant but unexpected promotion, most people in this position are not ready for it. However, once in a leadership role, the leader then develops through a process of growing into it (usually by hard work!), maturing in it by becoming wiser, making better decisions, and having sounder judgement but then sadly declining in the role.

The decline is often seen in the leader's becoming out of touch with both the followers and the needs of the situation. A classic example is that of Margaret Thatcher, whose dealings with her Cabinet showed an increasing authoritarianism before its members lost confidence in her. Had she forgotten how to listen?

Julius Caesar, Hitler, and Juan Peron all had lost contact with their people, were divorced from reality or had become obsessed with power long before their physical downfalls. There is a saying 'the good always die young'—it certainly applied to John F. Kennedy and Alexander the Great, so the question stands as to whether they too would have followed this process had they been allowed to continue.

The process in no way applies just to political leaders. In his book, Lee Iaccoca is scathing about Henry Ford Jr, who had lost all touch with why Ford Motors was successful and now saw up-and-coming executives as a threat. In the seventies the British trades union leadership pursued a doctrine of socialism that in time led to an infringement of the liberties of individual workers. Eventually their members saw through the nonsense but at the expense of the trades union movement itself.

So, let us embark on a more personal journey of discovery. The object of the discovery is leadership, we will examine the process of birth, growth, maturation, and decline, all in terms of what it means to you—your WIFMs!

The next chapter, although ostensibly about the birth of leadership, is very much about discovering the leader in you.

Your WIFMs from this chapter

- How many of the descriptions of leaders (good *and* bad) apply to you?

- Have you identified which parts of your job are leadership tasks and are you devoting sufficient time to them?

- Can you decide where you should be leading from (front, middle, or rear) given the demands of the situation you find yourself in?

- Which of the four leadership styles seems to be the closest to the one you usually adopt? Can you experiment by using another style?

- Can you identify the task clearly and work out how to accomplish it through the team and though individuals?

- Do you ever consider communicating with the passion and emotion you really feel? Is it worth trying to do so and observing the results?

- Where do you consider yourself to be on the continuum of birth, growth, maturation, and decline? How do you consider you can grow as a leader?

Knowing and valuing yourself

Self love—or self respect?

Leaders need to have self-esteem and this is very different from self-love. Self-esteem is based on an understanding of one's own personality and an acceptance of both its strengths and limitations.

It is crucial therefore to understand the difference between self-love and self-understanding; the former leads to narcissism and self-interest, neither of which is profitable to anyone. On the other hand, self-knowledge can be a very positive force for the good. But why is it important and how does it connect to valuing yourself or to having self-esteem, as it is more commonly known?

In Chapter 1 we examined a number of attributes and definitions of leadership and considered the sorts of behaviour that might well be found in people who were generally considered to be 'good' leaders. A degree of self-analysis is important and self-knowledge is one of the starting points in the process of the growth of leadership.

This chapter is about self-esteem and about self-understanding; an understanding of who you are, your strengths, your weaknesses, your hopes, and your fears. From this understanding can come either an acceptance and a valuing of what you are or, on the other hand, a desire to change into something closer to what you want to be. Both the acceptance and the positive striving for self-improvement are healthy and lead to self-respect. It is when there is no self-respect or a flawed self-image that people are most likely to be weak leaders, power mad, or just simply bad leaders.

Consequences of poor self-esteem

History is littered with leaders who caused havoc because they were trying to compensate for some personal inadequacy of which they were probably not fully aware. Hitler was a prime example, but more recently the late Richard

Nixon allowed the Watergate fiasco to happen because of a paranoid fear of losing. Was this because of a sense of personal inadequacy? In the realms of business, Robert Maxwell bullied and cheated his way to increased power and wealth until he finally toppled, but not before he had ruined many a life as well as his own. What drove him? It cannot simply have been the desire for more money.

Flawed behaviour can also often be seen further down the organization. Most people can cite examples of managers who exhibited very strange behaviour as bosses, and most will say that these individuals either had no understanding of themselves or that they were driven to act in a bizarre fashion by the realization of some personal inadequacy. The worst boss that I ever worked for, who had recently suffered a sideways move, had no confidence that he could do the job and chose to see subordinates as a threat rather than as people who could help him achieve his aims. As a result, his department was staggeringly uncreative and his staff both feared and despised him.

Avoiding the pitfalls

So how does one avoid these traps? A level of self-knowledge and self-respect is always important, no matter what the situation. However, when placed in a leadership role it becomes vital. Shakespeare stated that: 'some men are born great, some achieve greatness, and some have greatness thrust upon them.' Much the same can be said of leadership, and it is when leadership is thrust upon you in the form of additional responsibility or an unexpected promotion that this saying strikes closest to home and individuals most need to assess their talents and to start to value what they believe they can contribute to the role.

Growing confidence

An important first step to becoming a leader, or growing into the role, lies in achieving a realistic idea of what is required and then understanding that it is well within the scope of your talents to meet these requirements. The thinking process in the first step may go as follows:

1. Understand what leadership is and the leadership requirements of the job that you are faced with. In other words, how much of the job is about leading people.

2. Assess yourself. Think about the strengths you can bring to bear in the role and how you can capitalize on them. Recognize your weaknesses and consider how you can ensure that their effects are minimized or not taken advantage of by others.

3. Think about *what* it is that you need to do to be an effective leader.

4. Analyse *how* you are going to do these things.

5. Consider the obstacles and how they will be overcome. Get ready to start.

This may appear to be an oversimplification and, of course, it is never quite that easy. However, so many people invent obstacles for themselves that virtually guarantee that they will fail. These obstacles are embedded in a lack of self-belief or self-value. The obstacles need to be examined and destroyed as they stand in the way of so many people being able to realize their full potential—not just as leaders, but as people.

Overcoming the obstacles

It is in the process of inventing reasons why we should not succeed that many of us are at our most creative. Sometimes we go to elaborate lengths to dream up excuses why we should not step out and take the risk of trying to succeed ('I'm too busy' or, 'It wouldn't work if I tried doing it, anyway!'). But often these thought processes operate at a more subliminal level, although this does not make their influence any less powerful.

The name given to the subliminal process of convincing yourself that it is not worth changing, or making the effort, is that of having 'implicative dilemmas' or in layman's language 'payoffs'. It is worth a closer examination and perhaps the examination itself may help you identify some of your own payoffs.

To start we must imagine that there is a situation that we want to change, it may be something about ourselves or it may be a situation in which we find ourselves. Either way, to bring about the change requires making fairly radical changes to our approach or way of thinking and implies a level of risk.

The payoff

The thought process runs as follows: I decide that I want change. Or do I? It is true that I complain about my present situation and may well refer to it as the 'complaint'. But do I in fact see or use the 'complaint' as a convenient excuse for not achieving change?

I may actually consider that there are disadvantages associated with changing and then consciously or unconsciously add up the advantages associated with the complaint: 'The present situation may not be perfect but is not all bad and at least by maintaining it I don't have to face the challenge of the change.'

So, in the end, the disadvantages of or fear of change may outweigh any push for change and keep you from properly working towards achieving it. You have, therefore, trapped yourself in an implicative dilemma and the payoff is that you do not have to face up to the challenges of the change.

If this sounds a bit abstract, perhaps the following sad story may help illustrate it.

PAYOFFS—A TRUE STORY

There was once a girl in Holland who came from a solid middle-class background. Her parents never encouraged her to train for a career as it was always assumed that she would marry well and that her husband would provide for her.

In the fifties this was not such an unreasonable assumption as it would be considered today, and sure enough a man did come along and propose to her. Unfortunately, her parents strongly opposed the marriage as they felt the young man was unsuitable and swore that if she were to marry him they would cut her off for life.

Ignoring these threats, the girl married the man and bore him a child. Shortly after that her husband lived up to his parents-in-law's misgivings and deserted his wife and baby daughter. The poor woman was now in a terrible situation; her parents would not take her back, she could not work with the infant, and she was penniless. Of course Holland has a sophisticated social security system and she was soon housed and on social assistance. The social services, however, told her that they expected her to find work, any work, as soon as the baby was older.

Shortly after this something strange happened. For no apparent reason the young woman developed a large and painful ulcer on her leg. The doctors treating it were mystified, and even more so when the ulcer failed to respond to treatment. Eventually she was diagnosed as chronically unwell and placed on social security on an indefinite basis. It was very unpleasant having the ulcer, but was it preferable to facing up to the challenges of being trained as a semi-skilled worker and having to find work in a factory? Was the payoff for having the ulcer the let-out from work?

For some could the payoff of not rising to the challenge of trying to take on the role of leader be that it is comfortable and undemanding not doing so? Once again it comes down to a matter of making choices and of wanting to develop skills of leadership.

We could look at it another way.

Leadership is overcoming the payoff

A few years ago a survey in the USA asked some 90 top business leaders what they considered were the qualities required of an effective leader. They highlighted the following:

- Persistence

- Self-knowledge

- Willingness to take risks

- Willingness to accept losses

- Commitment

- Willingness to accept challenges

- Consistency

- Ability and desire to learn (from a wide range of sources)

It is interesting that they did not mention *charisma* and the fact that they did not do so is good news for the aspiring leader. The word 'charisma' is in itself probably responsible for more people deciding not to make the effort to become a leader than any other. By implication it refers to unobtainable, mystical qualities that you may be lucky enough to be born with but which you have no hope of attaining any other way. This is *not* the view of this book!

An examination of the qualities highlighted in the survey reveals that they are not so much qualities as things that we can *choose* to be or decisions about our behaviour that we can choose to make. The steps to leadership therefore are conscious and purposeful. There is no 'payoff' in not taking them! Take the steps and the qualities will reveal themselves!

THE QUALITIES EMERGE—AN ALLEGORICAL STORY

The following story, although just a fairy tale, illustrates this argument better than any other I know. It is familiar but surprisingly powerful.

Dorothy is in a fix. A tornado has just carried her out of her familiar surroundings into a strange and disconcerting land. She must find a way home. Eventually she is told that the only person who can help her is the wonderful Wizard of Oz and she sets off on the yellow brick road to find him.

On her way she meets some strange beings. There is the lion who is a coward and who desperately wants to have courage. There is the man of straw who has no brain and who would love to be intelligent, and then there is the tin man who is desperate to have a heart and to be able to feel emotion. To each of them Dorothy says, 'Come with me to the wonderful Wizard of Oz, he will give you courage, a brain or a heart'. And so, they set off down the yellow brick road to find the Wizard.

Of course when they do, they find that the Wizard is a complete sham and that he can do nothing for them. However, in subsequent adventures the lion shows great courage, and the man of straw great intelligence and wisdom, while the tin man finds that he has deep wells of emotion within him.

For each of them it was there all along. All it needed was for them to stop telling themselves that they could not be that way in order to start finding the qualities within. If you think that citing fairy stories is a bit far-fetched in an adult book on leadership, then it is worth stressing that fairy stories do reflect life and are full of wisdom. How else could they have lasted so well?

This line of thinking is born out in a number of different philosophies. Christian teaching proclaims that the Spirit of God is in us and that by believing that it is there the Christian can achieve great things. If a religious approach does not attract you, then try this philosophy. In parts of South East Asia many consider that each and every human being is already a champion and capable of greatness. Why? Well there is a logical answer; we are all the product of the single sperm that won the race to fertilize the egg and in doing so beat millions of others to do so. If that is not being a champion, then what is?

The leader within

Whichever approach you favour, one thing is definitely true. Many people's talents to be themselves or to be leaders have been submerged by a lifetime of other people's put-downs. These may have come about at school or through the family; perhaps as a result of the taunts of bullies or simply as a result of the low expectations of other people. Whatever the source, the result is usually the same: lack of confidence, lack of self-belief. But this can be overcome and in doing so the individual can find the leader within.

SIMON WESTON—A FORMULA FOR STEPPING OUT

A particularly moving example of this discovery taking place in real life can be seen in the example of Simon Weston, the Falklands war veteran who was so badly burned and scarred. He was eventually discharged from the army as he was considered to be too badly disabled to continue in it. Weston then sank into a morass of bitterness and self-pity and continued in that state for some considerable time, until he eventually emerged to head up charities dealing with disadvantaged children and to spread a message of hope to other scarred and mentally brutalized people. Simon Weston had emerged from the stagnancy of despair into becoming a leader and an example to many. What was the process for him?

Weston's story as told by him is simple and direct. It can also apply to any of us who are not stepping out to realize the leadership, or any other potential, in our lives.

What shocked him out of immobility was the realization that he was hiding behind his affliction. It had become a good excuse for not trying to do anything.

He had talked himself into a form of implicative dilemma! After that the steps to self-healing and then self-discovery began to fall into place with a sort of inevitable logic. As described to a conference of life insurance consultants, they were as follows:

1. Believe in yourself and that you are 'OK' no matter what your disadvantages may be.

2. Accept that complacency is an obstacle to self-belief and success.

3. Regrets are 'cop outs' and have no place in the process of your advancement.

4. There is only one standard to aim for and that is the best.

5. If you have problems and you feel bad about them then accept that nobody can cope with the misery for you, you have to do it yourself. The only help that works in the long term is self-help.

6. If there is adversity, *use it!* Decide that you are going to beat it and be on your own side.

After applying this formula of purposeful self-help and development, Simon Weston found to his surprise that he had become a more sophisticated, purposeful, and confident person than the young soldier he had been before that fateful day in the Falklands. A leader had been born and the same process can work for others.

Continuing the birth

In Chapter 1 a process of birth, growth, maturation, and decline of leadership was identified. Of course, once the birth has begun it must be continued, and perhaps the main difference between this birth and normal childbirth is that while the child cannot help in the process, the nascent leader most certainly can. So how can this be done?

There are certain crucial activities that need to be accomplished and some specific qualities that need to cultivated: they are in fact interdependent. The other key element that at least needs to be appreciated is that of power. But first the activities and qualities.

A helicopter overview, a quality of leadership

Emergent leaders need to be able to take an objective and dispassionate view of the overall situation in which they operate. This overview is some-

Figure 2.1   Helicopter overview.

times known as the 'helicopter view' and the insights it can give are known
as the 'helicopter effect'.

What it is describing is the fact that the leader has managed to remove
him or herself from the frantic rush and bustle of the situation and has
taken a detached view of the proceedings, enabling more clarity of thought
and better decision-making. The clearest description of the benefits of
taking a detached helicopter view of proceedings, especially when there are
a lot of problems besetting the situation, can be shown by an examination
of Figure 2.1.

Here a man is standing in the middle of a thick forest. The forest ends at a
small stream which becomes a lake and beside the lake are two buildings.
One building is a church with a bell and the other is a house with a
telephone line to the nearest town. Hovering above the forest is a woman
in a helicopter. The man and woman have totally different perspectives.

For example, the man can describe exactly what it is like to be in the
forest, he can describe the different types of trees that there are, he can tell
you what sort of animals there are in the forest and can probably even
describe the smell of the resin from the pine trees. The woman in the
helicopter could describe none of these details but could inform the
enquirer that there was a large expanse of forest down there with a lake at
its edge and a church and house with telephone wires leading from it
beside that lake. When it comes to describing the forest the man is at a

considerable advantage over the woman, however the balance of advantage changes dramatically when a problem develops. There is a forest fire!

Now all the man knows is that there is a fire but he is blinded by smoke and cannot see that if he were to run south for a short distance he would be safe. In fact a number of choices would be open to him. If he were a short-term thinker he could jump into the lake and be safe, if he took a longer term view he could run into the church and ring its bell for assistance, and if he were 'deeply into high tech' he could go into the house and use its telephone.

The woman in the helicopter could have told him all of this if only they had been able to communicate with one another. What the emergent leader needs to be able to do is to be in the forest among all the detail and activity for some of the time but then be able to join the woman in the helicopter when necessary, especially when problems abound. Perhaps what is needed is a 'Beam me up, Scotty' machine (for all Star Trek devotees!).

The challenge for the emergent leader is how to develop this ability to leap from the depths of the forest to the hovering helicopter. In fact, the mental and sometimes physical movement can allow problems to be seen in a different light and, for the leader, can enable the frame of mind to develop that permits a challenging of the status quo. It was not for nothing in the thought-provoking film *Dead Poets Society* that the poetry teacher made the pupils stand on their desks in order to look at poetry and the world differently, and not for nothing that at the end of the film that the boys stood on their desks again to show the outgoing teacher that, despite his dismissal, his lessons had not been forgotten.

A most telling example of the helicopter effect, or rather non-use of the helicopter, came in a quote from Prime Minister John Major who, in the middle of his government's crisis over insensitive handling of proposed pit closures in October 1992 said, 'We were perhaps too close to the detail.' He added that his cabinet simply did not realize the shock that would be caused by announcing all the pit closures in one fell swoop.

Boarding the helicopter

A method that can help you make the jump into the helicopter is that of examining the *demands*, *constraints*, and *choices* in the leadership situation that is facing you. This model was developed by Rosemary Stewart in *Choices for the Manager* and although it is principally aimed at helping managers to re-examine managerial work, it is of equal value in allowing new leaders to appraise the situation, as well as aspects of their characters in relation to the situation at hand.

Demands, constraints, and choices facing the leader

We will first look at demands, constraints, and choices in terms of managerial work and then branch out to place them in a leadership context.

Demands

In any job there will be those things that you must do; these are the 'musts'. If you do not do these things then sooner or later you will be reprimanded or fired; they are the nub of the job as it applies to you. Examples of demands might be:

- Meet deadlines
- Work to budget
- Appraise your staff fairly
- Answer queries
- Ensure quality of product
- Achieve profit targets
- Motivate your staff

Constraints

These are those things that make it harder for you to meet the demands. All jobs have constraints and it could be argued that it is because of constraints that organizations employ managers. They need people who can think creatively and use authority to obtain results despite the constraints. Examples of constraints might be:

- Low budgets
- Untrained staff
- What the competition is doing
- Time
- Inappropriate technology
- Lack of motivation
- Internal politics

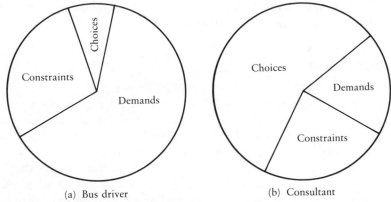

(a) Bus driver   (b) Consultant

Figure 2.2   Demands, constraints, choices.

■ Quality of information

■ Misdirection

Choices

These are the ways that the manager can elect to 'bust' the constraint. In fact it is the use of choice that is the characteristic of most management jobs. Therefore we must look at some of the choices and choice words that are open to the manager. These may be:

■ Ignore

■ Do differently

■ Select

■ Prefer

All jobs are a mixture of demands, constraints and choices. Some jobs have very high levels of demands, some constraints, and little scope for choice. An example of such a job might be a bus driver. Other jobs have a low level of demand in them but many constraints and a far higher area of choice. An example of such a job might be a management consultant.

It is possible to represent the way a job is constituted diagrammatically by slicing it up into its different elements rather like a cake. Thus Figure 2.2 illustrates (a) the bus driver's job with its low level of choice and (b) the management consultant's job with its completely different configuration. It follows that some people will be happy in the first job but would not be able to cope with the level of choice and discretion implied in the second. The opposite of course will also be true.

Using the model

So now for the ascent into the helicopter. Knowing the demands, constraints, and choices that are facing you and then acting on the areas of choice are a vital part of the nature of managerial work argues Rosemary Stewart. It can also be argued that a knowledge of the demands of your leadership role, the constraints that are within you that may now be preventing you from fully meeting these demands, and the choices that are open to you both in terms of self-development and of immediate positive action are the keys to growing effective leadership. Alternatively, analysing the demands and then realizing that you already have what it takes to meet them is another step in finding the leader within you.

But what are the demands of the leader's role you may well ask? Is it just a matter of selecting a variety of the behaviours listed in Chapter 1? If that is the case how do I choose from them? Do they apply to every situation no matter what its demands may be and no matter what constraints I feel there may be within me? No, it is not that simple (or should one better say complicated?).

What the demands–constraints–choices model can do is help leaders examine their situations objectively, and then examine their own strengths and weaknesses in relation to it. They must then choose the most appropriate leadership behaviour to match it. Here is an example.

THE NEW GENERAL MANAGER

Eve is a newly appointed general manager in a predominantly male engineering environment. The job is a bigger one than she has ever held before and to complicate matters her male predecessor, who was popular even though he had allowed certain business priorities to slip, is still on the premises, albeit now demoted and working in a different area.

Despite Eve's desire to succeed there are a number of risks, and at the end of her first week in the new job Eve sits down to analyse the demands, constraints, and choices facing her in both job and personal leadership terms. Her overview of the situation might well emerge as follows.

Demands:

- Make an impact.

- Ensure profits are made.

- Please customers and other stakeholders.

- Improve the business in general terms.

- Motivate staff.

- Take controlled risks when necessary.

- Be prepared to introduce change.

- Generate trust among the staff.

- Be strong when necessary.

- Be proactive.

- Send the right messages to staff.

- Emphasize need for shared values: trust, quality, etc.

- Earn respect, rather than demand it.

These demands not surprisingly incorporate a mixture of personal and business demands and meeting them will not be easy.

Constraints:

- The culture of the organization.

- Expectations of others.

- Potential lack of respect.

- Her own lack of confidence.

- Suspect motivation of some colleagues.

- Her own inexperience.

- Possible subversion by predecessor.

- Other people's fear of change.

The list of course might be a lot longer but already, by examining what Eve may perceive as the demands and constraints of both herself and the situation facing her, we may get clues as to the choices she faces.

Choices:

- Involve others in making decisions and implementing new ideas.

- Be open and honest with others.

- Show self-respect and also respect others.

- Do not conform to an expected role. Be individual.

- Communicate frequently and hold meetings.

- Trust other people.

- Allow other people to make decisions, but

- Be strong when necessary.

In the short term Eve made a remarkable start and overcame the disadvantages both of being a woman in a predominantly male environment and also of having her predecessor still on site. In the longer term her success was severely threatened by the fact that she forgot one of the demands that she had initially identified. Her success began to go to her head and she became arrogant, now starting to demand respect from others rather than trying to earn it. It needed counselling and further self-examination to pull her back from the brink.

The extra elements of leadership—a key word

In the end Eve needed just that little bit extra to make her fully successful and that extra element was wisdom. Wisdom is one element of what could be called the key to self-knowledge and self-respect and therefore the key to a positive and healthy approach to being a leader.

This key is found in the following mnemonic WIST. The letters stand for:

W *Wisdom*   This is nothing to do with intelligence. In fact it is sometimes hard to find wisdom and intelligence existing in the same person. Wisdom is about making the right decision. It is being able to sort out the truth from the jumble of contradictory information facing you. The wise do not allow themselves to be rushed, but take the time to consider problems properly. Having wisdom is about being objective and, while still feeling emotions, not allowing the emotions in a situation to interfere with the choice of the best course of action.

There are two other sides of wisdom. The first involves other people. A wise man or woman is a good judge of other people, they know what they are looking for in others and recognize it when they see it. They build the best teams because they have deliberately set out to do so on the basis of thought and insight. *Insight?* Well, perhaps insight is not the best word for it; although wise people will have insight into what motivates others. I prefer to call this talent 'intuition'. This in turn is a difficult concept to describe but ignore it at your peril.

A useful definition of intuition is short-circuited logic. We often think that something will happen or that someone will do something and cannot explain why we think this. Yet when we are proved to be right we are not at all surprised. There may be vestiges of good old-fashioned animal instinct in being intuitive; we look at someone and pick up messages about their feelings or intentions from their body language on a semi-primeval level. Intuition therefore may be deep-seated within us and arguably all humans have it, although many may dismiss intuitive thoughts as being illogical and in so doing do themselves a gross disfavour. Warren Bennis calls our intuition the 'inner voice' and urges us to listen to it. Sound advice indeed!

Growing wisdom within you then means doing a great deal of listening. Listening to what others are saying to you but even more to what the inner voice then starts to tell you. Wise judgement should then follow.

I   *Integrity*   This is easier to explain than wisdom as it involves fundamental principles. These principles govern the way that we deal with each other, the quality of what we say to each other, and the overall way that we do business. In short, it is about being truthful and not cheating one another. The sad fact nowadays is that so many values that used to be quite clear-cut are now devalued by being cloaked in grey. What is right? What is just?

The answer to questions like these is that it is wrong to lie, it is wrong to cheat (and is cheating not just another word for stealing?). If leaders embark on this course of action then it is not surprising if their followers lose their trust in them.

An acid test of whether an action infringes your personal sense of integrity comes in the old saying: 'Do unto others as you would have them do unto you'. If you would not like to be dealt with in that way then do not do it to other people. This is sound pragmatic advice and does not stop you from making the hard decision about people. You may still have to demote or dismiss people and both they and others will still respect you. However, lie to them about it and you have probably destroyed your credibility as their leader forever.

Once a colleague asked me to be part of a very dubious set of proceedings that he was initiating and which involved 'doing the dirty' on a third party. He added, 'Don't worry, you can trust me!' Was this really now possible?

S   *Sensitivity*   Closely allied to intuition, sensitivity is the ability to put yourself into the other person's shoes, to imagine what they may be thinking about at a given moment, and then to take the right action based on that imaginative guesswork. We often talk about being sensitive to the situation, and this sensitivity can lead you on to saying or doing the right thing. People respect that ability but seldom respect the insensitive person who has not picked up the nuances of the situation and therefore blunders in causing mayhem and upsetting all concerned. Once again, most of us have the capacity to be sensitive but we often do not allow ourselves to be so, either by not allowing ourselves time to analyse the person or situation, or by blatantly putting *ourselves* first.

The trap, of course, is that the person who is shown to have acted insensitively loses self-respect and the respect of others. There are occasions that I can recall when I said or did something insensitively that still make me cringe several years later! So, being sensitive is much more than simply being emotional. It is about being smart.

A greater danger is discovering that you have acted in an insensitive way can lead to loss of self-confidence and from there potentially becoming the dangerous leader with something to prove.

T *Tenacity*   People who succeed do not give up easily. If everything in life were easy there would be little need for leaders. But as problems usually abound, both individuals and teams look for someone who will help them see it through and who will support them in difficulty.

Being tenacious means persevering and making your mind up to succeed. It requires energy but, in addition, a mental toughness that is different from the toughness shown by the strong negotiator or the strict supervisor.

The qualities that the development of tenacity require are resolution, determination, and a desire to finish successfully. Once again these qualities are not the sole province of Superman and Wonder Woman, they are parts of you that you can choose to develop.

So be *WISTful* and be *powerful*!

The WISTful leader is probably the one who has developed a secure power base. Therefore it is now necessary to examine the foundations of power in organizations.

Power

Power in organizations is a reality and one that has to be faced. Some use power like a blunt instrument while others who have it do not seem to know it.

Having a knowledge of the demands, constraints, and choices facing you and then acting 'WISTfully' will enhance your power but it is also necessary to understand where your power lies and what supports it.

In fact, power is a fascinating concept. We all have it to greater or lesser degrees but we do not all know where it comes from. Of course, the most obvious and unsubtle forms of power are easy to understand. The bully uses force, or the threat of it, successfully because the main lever is fear. 'If you do not do what I want, I am going to hurt you.' This threat is often used by managers in business in a thinly disguised format and, it is true, these people have power. But are they using or abusing it?

This form of power must be short-lived because the followers act out of fear rather than out of respect. When other people act on your wishes because they want to and because they respect your will rather than fear it, then you have *authority*.

The foundations of authority

In organizations, the leader's authority is made up of three different but complementary elements. Two of the elements depend on what you put into them. Similar to the demands of remembering the task, team, and individual, it is once again necessary to remember all three of these elements.

Positional authority

This is the authority that exists in the position or job that the leader has taken on. In an organization it is common to find that certain levels of job carry their own authority or kudos just because they are known to be senior, responsible positions. Thus, when a new jobholder moves into a senior position, other people decide that he or she must be 'impressive and responsible' simply because of the job, and give the respect due until the jobholder proves them wrong. At that stage the respect is withdrawn.

This works most powerfully when the jobholder moves in from outside the organization as an unknown quantity, but the theory still holds true for internal promotions.

When I worked for Ernst and Whinney (now Ernst and Young), a major firm of chartered accountants, the level of partner was the most revered target within the firm and I was quite often surprised at the organization's choice of people for this level. Although many of my colleagues were equally surprised, there was a general feeling that, as the position was so revered, the new jobholder must have qualities that most other people had failed to notice. In other words, the position had enough authority vested in it to guarantee the jobholder a 'honeymoon period' when they first started in it.

All honeymoons, however, come to an end and, as in all marriages, after that it is up to the individual. Consequently, the other two bases of authority are more important to you and more dependent upon you and what you do.

Personal authority

Think back to Chapter 1 and consider your thoughts on the best and worst bosses. It is unlikely that you respected your worst bosses, although you may have feared them. Consequently, people who do not act fairly, reasonably, or decisively as individuals within the role soon begin to erode their positional authority. At the time of writing the premiership of John Major was being called into question as a result of questions about his character—the honeymoon was well and truly over.

Expert authority

This is the third foundation stone of the leader's authority. Whatever the business, the leader must understand how it works. This does not mean to say that the leader must understand every bit or angle of the business; this is increasingly difficult these days and to do so might well interfere with helicopter vision. However, a good general understanding of the business and the environment it operates in is essential. Without it, clear decision-making becomes difficult and, what is more dangerous, other people begin to mistrust those decisions.

Tom Peters in *In Search of Excellence* urged readers to go in for *MBWA—management by wandering around*. This has a number of benefits; it shows other people that you are interested and also keeps you informed and aware of what is going on. One of the most frequent criticisms of declining leaders is that they have lost touch. In other words, they did not work on their expert authority.

It is clear that the authority of the position is upheld by the other forms of authority and that these foundations are both earned by the leader as well as granted by the leader's colleagues and subordinates.

Both elements of personal and expert authority are something that the leader can grow through work and persistence. Consequently, finding the time to reflect and relax is a vital prerequisite to the individual's development and growth as a leader.

Time is also vital in enabling the emergent leader to move from the areas of self-knowledge and discovery to the task of constructing the guiding vision which will be the subject of Chapter 3.

Summary

Both the elements of personal and expert authority are something that you, the emergent leader, can do something about. They both require work and persistence but those are things that the leader should not fear. In addition, a good level of self-esteem and self-knowledge should clarify exactly where the effort is needed to support your power base.

But where do I find the time for all of this? How do I get myself into the right frame of mind to be objective about myself and to value myself? These are questions you may well be asking by now. Time to reflect as well as to relax is a vital prerequisite and we will examine how to find the time to do this in Chapter 3 when we move into the realm of visions.

Your WIFMs from this chapter

■ Have you considered the innate strengths that you can bring to bear to make you an effective leader?

■ What is stopping you from realizing your potential as a leader? Are you hiding behind any payoffs?

■ What do you need to overcome? Have you decided to do so?

■ Have you assessed the demands, constraints, and choices facing you?

■ How real are the constraints? Can they be challenged?

■ Have you considered the bases of your authority? What do you need to do to augment and legitimize your authority?

Conceiving, testing, and implementing your vision

The power of the vision

'I have a dream', proclaimed Martin Luther King, and his people cheered. At the same time, his enemies took fright and plotted against him. Such is the power of the leader's dream or vision.

But what is the vision? Why can it be so powerful and from where does it spring? At present, the word vision is in danger of being devalued through overuse. We tend to hear it used in all manner of contexts and it could end up like one of those many 'management' words such as 'proactive' and 'synergy' which are used everywhere and whose power and meaning are therefore largely lost.

The leader's vision of the future, or of what can be done with the present, is probably the key feature that transforms that person from being a manager who maintains and administers the status quo to a leader who mobilizes others to achieve change and improvement. It could be argued that it is the vision that gets the results, rather than the individual in the role of leader.

A LACK OF VISION

As a new and inexperienced personnel manager in the Plessey Company I took over from a respected predecessor who had managed the HR function very competently for over a decade before retiring. The department ran like clockwork as he had over the years found the best way to do just about everything.

After I had held the job for a few weeks my boss asked me what I was going to do with it, what changes I was going to make and what I saw as the future of the department. When I naively replied that everything seemed to run so smoothly that I hesitated to think of changes, he bluntly said that that was not good enough. I was expected to have a dream of what could be done with the function and that maintaining the status quo, no matter how comfortable that was today, was not what was needed for tomorrow!

So, the leader needs a vision, no matter how senior or junior that leader may be. But what *is* the vision?

Definitions

As stated already, an amusing but apt description of the vision is: 'Having a picture of the cathedral in your mind when you first start to mix the concrete.' This is useful because it sums up much about what the vision is, as well as what must come after it. We have our dream or ambition; it is something that is not immediately achievable and therefore work and effort are needed to turn that ambition into reality. We cannot achieve the ambition solely by our own efforts and so we must seek the support of others to help us get there. However it is not going to be an easy journey. At times the road is going to be long and hard and sometimes we may have to make sacrifices or put up with monotony.

If those others do not share the same exciting picture of what the cathedral will be like and share the same values that the building of it is both worth while and necessary, then they will perceive only the toil and hardship involved. Debatably then, the only way by which we can ensure that they continue to mix the concrete is through the use of fear or bribery.

A few examples may help to put some flesh on the bones.

Examples

Perhaps one of the leaders to use his vision in the most compelling of ways was Adolf Hitler. Here we have the case of a strange and disturbed individual who happened to have a picture in his mind of a new Germany. Wrapped up in this picture were many of his own ambitions, hurts, and resentments. The new Germany would have room for all 'real' Germans to live and prosper. It was going to be possible to recapture a glorious, although fantasy, past and if a prosperous minority of non-real Germans seemed to stand in the way, then of course there was a solution.

Unfortunately for the world, Hitler's own resentments sufficiently echoed those of a defeated and inflation-racked German people to give meaning and hope to sufficient numbers to sweep him into power.

Visions can work powerfully for nations, they can also transform businesses. The processes are not all that different.

THE NEW NAME—ACHIEVING THE CORPORATE VISION

An interesting example of a transforming vision can be seen in the work done in a financial services organization in the 1980s. This UK-based firm just happened to be the largest provider of venture capital in the City of London, it had helped pioneer a number of innovative schemes such as management buy-outs, and it also owned large-scale equity in a number of growing organizations. The name was Finance for Industry and the vast majority of the business community had not heard of it.

In fact it was so little known that this lack of visibility was actively restricting its growth. Unfortunately, those who did know of it often laughed when they saw the organization's name reduced to its initials, FFI. In the British armed forces FFI were the letters that were stamped on your medical card after you had completed a cure for one of the venereal diseases. The letters stood for 'free from infection', or in army vernacular, 'fit for intercourse!'

FFI's then chief executive was fully aware of the disadvantages of an outdated name and had a vision of the organization as taking an active and innovative lead in its chosen field. For this to happen it needed a new name and a new image, one that would more fully describe its role and excite potential clients. After lengthy consultations with public relations and image consultants the new name and image were revealed at a management conference at Gleneagles. The new name was *3i—Investors In Industry*.

Overcoming the obstacles

At first this announcement had a very mixed reception. The old guard objected to the name, stating that the organization would become confused with the tourist information service. Others, looking at the new zany logo, which had a drawing of an eye in it, proclaimed that it contained the evil eye and that people would be afraid to do business with the firm. For a time these objections and others of varying degrees of practicality or lunacy prevailed. Many, seeing a potential change to the balance of power in the organization, sought all forms of means of stopping or slowing the change process. Real leadership was called for and for a time the CEO, Jon Foulds, adopted a role of leading from the front.

Foulds embarked on an energetic timetable of visiting offices, talking to people at all levels, listening to them, explaining details more fully, and consistently pushing his message. He actively pushed the rationale of the change and stressed the benefits.

New methods of working were implicit in the changes so there were many concerns as well as ambitions to be dealt with. He was also tough. People swiftly found that sabotage of the plans was not acceptable and could be severely 'career regressive'. However, in the end, it was the leader's commitment, the repetition of the vision, and the passion for it that won the day.

It also won the day for the organization, which was able to obtain the visibility it deserved. It found a new high profile and a new reputation for innovation at a time of great change and opportunity in the City of London. In effect, the new visibility allowed *3i* to adopt publicly the leading role that it had, in practice, held for many years.

Here the CEO had the advantage of being able to call on the help of a large administration to help him achieve his vision. It can also be done by an individual with equal effect as the following example shows.

Achieving an individual vision: case study

The background

Although it is a modern example, the start of the vision lies with Maurice Buckmaster of SOE in the early 1940s.

In order to fulfil Hitler's warped vision for a new Europe, Germany occupied France. That bit of history is well known and documented. What is less well known is what subsequently took place in various regions of the country.

As the job of maintaining the war effort became harder for Germany, Hitler's regime found it necessary to deport young people forcibly from the countries they had invaded in order to work in factories in Germany. One region that was particularly singled out for this policy was the Jura region in South East France. In doing this, they made a grave error of judgement as the bulk of the young men, rather than submit to forcible deportation, quite literally took to the hills.

For some time these fugitives were content merely to avoid capture, but by 1943, under the leadership of a French army officer called Ramon Petit, they began to organize themselves. The Maquis had been born. Later they were joined by a British officer, Richard Heslop, codenamed Xavier, who further organized them as a fighting force and who had a link to Buckmaster in London.

It soon became evident to Xavier that the Maquis could be little more than a nuisance to the German occupiers unless they were properly armed and resourced. Clandestine radio messages were passed in which Xavier begged Buckmaster to send arms and supplies so that the Maquis could conduct an effective armed resistance.

Buckmaster eventually sent a Major Patterson who parachuted into the Jura to inspect the Maquis and assess its readiness for battle. Patterson spent some weeks clandestinely touring the region inspecting the fugitive army for its readiness to start a major campaign of sabotage and unrest.

Repression continues

Things hotted up, the Gestapo shot the local doctor, Emile Mercier after someone had informed on him, and unrest grew. Patterson escaped to neutral Switzerland with Ramon Petit and sent a message to Buckmaster urging him to send arms and supplies in large numbers to the Maquis.

This took place shortly afterwards when Flying Fortresses, instead of dropping bombs, dropped masses of arms to the awaiting Maquis. It was now ready to answer Churchill's call to set Europe ablaze, and this it did with gusto, helping to tie down thousands of German soldiers who should have been moved north to help defend Normandy.

If you now visit the Jura area in South East France you will be struck by the number of roadside monuments to the Maquisards who fell in clashes with the *Wehrmacht*.

But what has this history lesson to do with a modern vision and its realization?

After the liberation of France, the de Gaullists came to power and a time of confusion and vengeance ensued. Many de Gaullists resented the more active part that the Maquis had played in the liberation and astoundingly embarked on a strategy of reparation against its members. Ramon Petit was jailed as politically undesirable and Heslop was given 48 hours to leave the country. Some gratitude!

In fact, since that time the 'Gaullists' have continued to play down the contribution of the Maquis (and its teamwork with SOE) to the liberation of France. That is where this individual vision really begins.

Birth of a vision

Emile Mercier had been shot by the Gestapo as they were taking him from Nantua to Bourg-en-Bresse for 'interrogation'. At the time his son, Pierre, was one year old and he grew up never having known his father. Forty years passed, Pierre Mercier grew up to be a flamboyant, expansive character and became the local osteopath. Memories of the war faded and Nantua went on its way as a small provincial town. Many veterans of the Maquis, however, did not forget the Resistance and the central part that the region had played in it. Pierre Mercier grew up to feel the same and felt it passionately.

Out of this passion grew an idea. This idea linked a commemoration of the activities of the Maquis and of SOE with a dynamic new project designed to add benefit to the sleepy town. He decided to found a museum to commemorate the Maquis. It would form a central focus of the town and it would be the best museum of its kind in France. That was the vision, and it was to become the driving force in both his and the town's lives.

Communicating the vision

There then followed a time of feverish activity. Mercier needed to communicate the idea far and wide, he had to get the veterans on his side and persuade them to back his idea, he needed premises for the museum, and he needed exhibits. Above all, he needed the wholehearted commitment of the local population and authorities.

Bit by bit the idea took shape. He found allies in some prominent citizens and persuaded the authorities to donate the old town jail (a substantial building) as the site for the museum. Many disapproved, but he repeated his vision, its benefits, and the passion he felt for it time and time again.

Contacts with the SOE veterans' club in London produced more information as well as artifacts and slowly the whole town became infected with enthusiasm for the project as the museum started to take shape. It became far more than a memorial to the past, it became a focus of civic pride. The vision did not end there; as it grew into reality within the converted jailhouse it gained further momentum. As new enthusiasts helped embellish it by donating mementos, documents, uniforms, and even captured German weapons, they too were captured by the spirit of what the museum represented. To this day the museum continues to grow and flourish.

If you visit the *Museé de la Deportacion et de la Resistance* in Nantua you will be amazed at the scope and quality of a small town's museum that in many ways is more ambitious and more creative than the Imperial War Museum in London. You may even see Pierre Mercier working there as, once achieved, all visions require maintenance and improvement.

The example of *3i* and the case of Pierre Mercier were two very different situations, but some remarkable similarities exist. What was there in common and what can we learn from them? They show that it is possible to list the essential steps in vision realization.

Essential steps

1. There was a motive and it was born out of the wish to *improve* or *change* a situation.

2. The central characters *permitted themselves to dream* and allowed the idea to grow.

3. They *felt passionately* about the validity of their dream. This strength of feeling came about because they could see the impact of the vision in the long term and why it would benefit people or situations in the future.

4. They *communicated their vision*, again and again. However, the message had to have validity or meaning for those to whom it was communicated.

5. By doing this, they *influenced* other people and then *supported* those who were now on their side.

6. They *allowed others to contribute* creatively to their vision.

7. They *listened* to the comments of others but were not swayed from their central theme.

8. They *exhibited great energy* and always pressed ahead with implementation plans.

9. Once the central theme of the vision was achieved, they realized that the real work had scarcely started and communicated this fact to others in a way that motivated them.

Links to a business situation

These essential steps transfer easily into a business situation and although the following language may sound rooted at CEO level, it can and should be used by people at all levels of an organization.

1. Any business must have a *mission* and this is usually expressed in a concise, clear-cut statement. The mission statement must describe the organization's reason for existence. It is the 'what we are here to do' statement. The mission is not the vision, although the vision for the organization is usually concerned with fulfilling the mission in some special way.

2. The *vision* is about what we are going to do with the business in the future. What are we going to look like in five years' time? If the vision is not clearly articulated then progress over the next stages will probably be impaired.

3. After the vision must come *objectives and goals*. They help both pose and answer the following questions. How can we tell whether we are achieving the vision? What targets can we set along the way and how will we know that we have successfully met them?
   If we can ensure that the objectives that we set for people are consistent with a vision that hopefully has meaning for them, then they are far more likely to work towards it in a purposeful way and see the achievement of targets as stepping stones on the way to its realization.

4. The strategy is about *how* the steps on the road to realizing the vision are achieved and it identifies the overall direction of those steps. There will be more about the leader as strategist in Chapter 10 but suffice it here to say that once again, the strategy should be the servant of the vision, so a failed strategy need not mean that the vision is worthless. Failure may say more about the operation of the strategic planning department!

Figure 3.1   Brand *X* dominates the High Street.

The essential steps and the business definitions are the tools that leaders use within a business context to achieve their dreams.

Expressing and testing the vision

For a vision to excite, for it to capture hearts as well as minds, for it to give meaning to why people work, it must be expressed clearly and reflect their values. Sometimes the leader may want to change the prevailing values. When this is the case, the vision must be expressed even more clearly, convincingly, and dramatically.

On one of the leadership programmes I help run we have 'vision expression exercises'. Delegates are asked to express their visions for their function as clearly as possible and then to submit them to testing questions from the rest of the group. They are encouraged to be as creative as possible.

The author of one vision worked in marketing for a drinks company. Her brand competed fiercely with other brands and one of the keenest battlegrounds was in the High Street—not in the big supermarket but in the small corner shop. Her vision, expressed in a simple drawing, was dramatic and challenging. It showed a High Street dominated by a huge can of her company's main product. The underlying message was that the competition would be eclipsed and the strap line was 'Brand *X* dominates the High Street'. (Figure 3.1)

Considerable planning and effort were implied in turning this vision into reality and the battle still continues. The first step in the offensive, however, was to duplicate the picture and to circulate it widely within the organization. It became a banner behind which the marketing offensive was launched.

Testing the vision

The marketing executive's vision was, during the programme, subjected to scrutiny and testing. Some of the questions posed went as follows:

1. Does the vision really illustrate what I want to achieve?

2. Is the vision relevant to my type of business?

3. Is the vision clear? Can it be communicated in a way that will convince and excite others?

4. How will the vision mobilize others? Are there any clues?

5. How will the vision be managed? How will it be translated into objectives that other people will want to adopt as their own?

6. Can the vision statement, or the essential picture it conjures up, be reflected in everything we do, be a yardstick for target-setting and a guide for even minor activities?

In order to prevent them from becoming 'pie in the sky', all visions should be subjected to such a battery of questions.

Why test?

As a result of these questions a business should be able to come up with a vision statement that dovetails neatly with its overall mission and which then percolates into a series of easily identifiable actions and targets.

The following example of a mythical IT consultancy shows how this can be done. The chief executive has completed the visioning process, subjected the vision to the vision test questions outlined above, and has now published the following statement in order to focus the minds of all staff. In effect, what the CE has done has been to think of the answer (what we want to see happen) and then thought of what will be required to get the business to that state.

THE MOTIVATIONAL STATEMENT

Turning the vision into action

Our *mission* is to achieve results for our clients through IT consultancy and the implementation of new systems for them.

Our *vision*, which is the starting point for all our plans, and which sums up all that we want for the business is: 'To be the leading international IT consultancy, providing demonstrable and quantifiable results for our clients.'

To share this vision and to ensure that we have a common understanding of its implications, I have defined the meaning of the words that have been used. This has been done in two ways:

1. Elements of the mission and vision

2. What the business will look and feel like when we achieve the vision

Elements of the mission and vision

- *Main Thrust*   To be the leading international IT consultancy providing demonstrable and quantifiable results for our clients.

- *Operation*   To operate as a group, thereby offering clients interdisciplinary services backed by the resources of our total organization both nationally and via our international network.

- *Development*   To invest in all forms of technical research and development to meet the needs of our clients and to ensure a strong and vital presence in each of our chosen markets.

- *Quality*   To pursue a policy of total quality to ensure our clients receive impressive results from our work. Quality of service, quality of staff, and quality of delivery.

- *People*   To provide exceptional careers and rewards for our people, to attract, retain, and develop acknowledged authorities in their chosen fields who will offer clients expertise of the highest order.

- *Performance*   To produce revenue growth and margins that will support the consultancy, sustain a high capital investment, fund research and development, enhance quality, and reward staff. All of this will guarantee the success of the business.

What the business will look and feel like

- *Leading*
  —We clearly address our clients IT needs.
  —A large proportion of our work is carried out for large multinational organisations and the top 500 in the world.
  —A significant number of our staff are acknowledged authorities in their fields.
  —We are ahead of our competitors in every way.
  —The media seek our opinion concerning IT development issues.
  —We make quality a top priority and people are proud to work for us.

—We are proud of our own systems and procedures and lead the way with them.

■ International

—We are regarded as the leading *international* IT consultancy.

—We achieve our planned level of operation in chosen countries.

—Most of our staff are able to work with clients in a second language.

—We will have a multinational, cross-cultural team of consultants who do not see themselves as bound to any one culture.

■ *Leading IT consultancy*

—We apply our expertise to address issues that our competitors cannot.

—We apply innovative, state-of-the-art solutions to client needs using skills drawn from all sources.

—Experts in IT and related disciplines want to spend part of their careers working with us.

—Extensive research and development support our work.

—The facilities and other support material are of the highest quality.

■ *Results*

—Our clients agree that we help them achieve the results that our competitors cannot.

—Our clients see these results as giving them tangible advantages against their competitors and therefore come to us because they want to win.

—The results of our work are permanent and creative. Clients stay with us because quality is guaranteed.

■ *Clients*

—We always put the client first.

—We work with the biggest, most prestigious and discerning.

—We do not waste our efforts by bidding for inappropriate work.

In quantifying the vision in that way the chief executive is challenging members of the organization as well as starting to develop a process by which targets can be set and progress towards them measured.

The vision is starting to move from a fairly general statement into something by which both departments and individuals can be assessed. Some may say that the CEO may be inviting trouble by spelling the vision out in that sort of detail; a broader, less concisely expressed vision may be safer. To say that, in effect, misses the point.

Visions have to become targets in themselves and in so doing must permeate all levels and affect the way that even minor jobs are done. From reading this vision statement, even the dullest employees should be able to pick up messages about what is expected of them, how they do their jobs, and how they treat the organization's clients.

One way of looking at it is to see the vision, the organization's strategy, and the daily work as being like the links of a chain. They are all connected and interdependent; break a link and the chain can fulfil no purpose!

In fact our imaginary CEO could decide to specify targets and account-abilities even more clearly. Revenue targets, market positions, degree of international spread, and proportion of income to be devoted to R&D can all be charted and spelt out in detail. From this, all responsible employees will be able to measure the organization's progress towards the vision at any given time as well as their own contribution to it. The very fact that a vision has been stated now implies action for all concerned.

Starting the visioning process

How do I start and where do I find the time? These are certainly reasonable questions. Unless you are prone to blinding flashes of genius then finding the time to go through the visioning process is vital.

This is not a book about time management, however, it is necessary to find the time to vision. Usually books on time management help readers to sort out their priorities and often break tasks down into three different types of priority:

- *Priority A*   These are tasks which are both important and urgent. If they are not done fast and well then the consequences will be severe.

- *Priority B*   These are tasks which are either important but not urgent or not important but urgent.

- *Priority C*   These tasks are neither important nor urgent and by implication should be ignored, delegated, or binned.

Regrettably, too many would-be leaders give the visioning process a C priority. This is totally wrong, as it is vital to have a clear and quantifiable picture of what you wish to achieve. Make visioning priority A, give it the same quality time as you would give to a more tangible activity. It is at least as important!

Seeking the vision

The process will vary from individual to individual. Many find it hard to sit down with the expressed intent of coming up with a vision for their business or department but, unless they are lucky enough to have had the vision seek them out, they had better plan to do some seeking themselves.

One general prerequisite seems to be that a relaxed mind is a more open and creative mind, so strive to be relaxed. Once again most of us have our own preferred ways of seeking relaxation. Some play music, others think some of their best thoughts while taking exercise, while others go in for yoga or meditation. Do what comes most easily for you, whether this be in the work environment or outside it. Many now choose to work at home when they want to devote time to high-quality thinking without interruption.

For those who want a quick and safe method of inducing mental relaxation, here is a way. Sit down comfortably, close your eyes and then talk yourself through the following scenario. This technique, and a variety of others, come from the growing field of stress reduction. It is called the temple of complete silence.

RELAXATION—A METHOD

Imagine that you are walking down a busy street. It is a hot day and people jostle you as you go. The air is full of the sound of traffic and there is movement and bustle everywhere. You pass a bookshop and see the books in the window. You pass a fishmongers and can actually smell the fish that are offered for sale.

Eventually you get to a narrow, shady alley and turn down it. Here all is quiet and peaceful, the buildings are old, quaint, and friendly. You pass an iron railing with a bicycle leaning against it. As you walk down the gentle incline of the alley you start to relax. Eventually you come to a large, dark building with an oak doorway. On the door is a brass plaque saying: 'This is the temple of complete silence. Enter.'

You enter and walk along a hall and down some steps until you find yourself in a large restful room, it has stained glass windows so the light is dim. The room has a large armchair. On a table in front of the armchair is a card and on it is written: 'Sit down, you may rest here as long as you wish.'

In fact by the time you have talked yourself into the armchair you are probably already in a state of relaxation. When you feel that you have relaxed there long enough, talk yourself back through the process until you find yourself back in the busy street again. You will be surprised at how relaxed and refreshed you feel when you open your eyes.

Just one word of warning. *Never* relax in this way when driving a car!

Once you are ready and relaxed allow yourself to start visioning. Some further guidelines to help get started may still be necessary as a means of helping you to focus on the right area.

FOCUSING GUIDELINES

These guidelines are quite short and not totally specific as the whole process is a very personal one and a prescriptive approach might be stultifying for some people:

1. What is the present situation? What are the problems? How could it be improved?

2. What would I really like to see happen to the business? Are these desires realistic?

3. Am I being totally open-minded in my thoughts or am I weighed down by unnecessary clutter, past resentments, or selfish thoughts?

4. How can what I want to see happen to the business solve its problems? If the vision does not solve problems and indicate a better situation ahead, is it valid?

Summary—your final commitment

When you have the basis of your vision laid out before you it is now necessary to make a firm decision to pursue it—to go for it! Implementation now must be the driving aim.

Once the decision to start implementing the vision has been made it should take hold of you and be a driving force in itself. If it does not become so then you should query whether it is really what you passionately wish to see happen. Warren Bennis in *On Becoming a Leader*, talks about the leader 'forging the future'. You must believe in the future that you are starting to forge as the strength of your belief, as well as your doubts, will be infectious.

Your WIFMs from this chapter

- Do you have a vision of what you want to achieve?
- Can you state, or picture, the vision clearly?
- Do you have a plan as to how best to communicate the vision?
- Are you willing to let others contribute to the formulation of your vision?
- Can you separate the vision from the mission and then further distinguish your objectives and goals?
- Does your vision stand up to scrutiny and testing?
- Have you allocated quality time to developing your vision?
- Do you feel passionately about the vision?

Leading the team

Definitions and validations

A definition of a team that seems to fit well is 'a group of people with a high degree of interdependence, geared towards the achievement of a task'. In this definition certain words really sum it all up.

It is 'a group of people' and if this group becomes too large it will find it hard to act as a cohesive unit. Indeed, sociological studies indicated that when a group exceeded seven it was liable to break down into subgroups. So it would appear that a management team, to work well together, should not be allowed to become too large. If that is something within your control as a leader it is a point well worth remembering.

Then, it is an interdependent group of people and the word 'interdependent' is vital. A group of people may accept that they all work for the same company but they may not accept that they are all dependent on each other's efforts. After all, what have the efforts of the Birmingham office got to do with me? It is involved with a different product line, they could close it and it would make no difference to my well-being. On the other hand, if one of my colleagues does exceptionally well, or badly, and it affects us both in the achievement of the task, then we are part of the same team.

The most obvious example to quote would be a sporting team, where one weak player can obviate all the hard work of others. However, it works equally powerfully at work. In the running of management training programmes a course may be running well until one of the tutors 'goofs', after that all the tutors have to work doubly hard to recoup the situation.

Finally there is the common task, whether it be a long-term or short-term one. Teams need tasks and objectives, and if they cannot identify any will either drift apart or invent some.

But are teams really necessary? The individualist might say that they get in the way of individual expression. Like them or not, teams appear to be an integral part of life. They are fundamental and necessary. At the dawn of creation mankind found it necessary to live, forage, and hunt in teams. Life was too hard and the animal kingdom too strong to permit survival without them. Perhaps 'man' had observed parts of the animal world and learnt from them. Wolves, for example, hunt in packs but the system they have designed involves far more than a mere rabble dashing hell for leather after its prey. They use a sophisticated system in which different members of the pack take over the role of lead runner, then other members join in the hunt at different points in the chase, thus ensuring that the pressure on the hapless quarry is unrelenting. In this way 'teams' of wolves can catch their prey, something that the lone wolf would find impossible to do.

A key fact about teams, therefore, is that they usually achieve more than any one individual within the team is able to achieve singly. Within teams leaders emerge, sometimes it is done through battles of strength or will: a mental (and sometimes physical) locking of horns. Often the leader is appointed by the organization with a specific remit to lead the team, and sometimes a leader is elected by the team from among its members. Whichever the case may be, there are a number of things of which you need to be aware if you are that leader.

Teams and organizations

In the nervous nineties organizations are changing fast and so is the environment in which they are forced to operate. Chapter 8 will look at the effects of change in more detail but for the purposes of this chapter, let us look briefly at what is happening to the structure of organizations.

Today, two commonly heard words are 'downsizing' and 'delayering'. The first is a cheap euphemism for getting rid of people while the second is far more positive.

EXAMPLE OF A LAYERED ORGANIZATION

In the late seventies I joined the Plessey Company; it was a large complex organization and typical of many in that era. It boasted a management structure with 12 grades of management between group CEO and junior manager.

Most people were comfortable with this structure; the organization recruited heavily from the ranks of the armed forces where observable hierarchies were the norm. It was easy to tell what grade a manager held because each grade held different badges of office. For example, at one grade you were given a carpet, at another a glass top to your desk, and everyone knew when you had reached one of the coveted senior grades as you received a company car and used the 'executive mess'. The head office took this to extremes with no less than three executive messes. I remember attending one management meeting during which we went in three different directions when lunchtime came round.

Fortunately, with delayering, the process of eliminating different levels of management, this type of structure is becoming increasingly rare. The implications for leaders within organizations are, however, significant.

With fewer layers the opportunity for teamwork increases. There is less hierarchy, and people can work together without having to be so aware of 'rank'. The very nature of so much work today, in facing the customer to deliver goods or services according to negotiated specifications, lends itself clearly to project working. Projects usually imply teams and so do a number of other work-based situations.

Insofar as it may fall within your scope of choice as to whether to set up a team to get results, here are some general guidelines for when teams may or may not be the right medium. Teams often work less well in situations that require quick and urgent activity where immediate results, perhaps of a fire-fighting nature, are needed and where the only approach to guarantee quick, although perhaps short-term, results is a non-team autocratic approach.

THE CRISIS—A NON-TEAM DECISION

In the warehouse of a scientific instrument and laboratory supply company called Griffin and George (now part of the Fisons Group) there was a major crisis. Owing to staff shortages and unworkable procedures it became almost impossible to get the goods out to satisfy clients. A management team tried to reach consensus on the right remedial actions and failed. Finally they agreed to give the whole problem and unlimited authority over to one member of that team.

The first thing that the manager did was to announce that all middle managers under the age of 30 would spend the next 4 weeks working in the warehouse to eliminate the log jam. There were howls of protest but it happened, and many of those managers soon came up with ideas to make the warehouse systems more efficient. Another result was unexpected team-building between the young managers and the warehouse operatives; but that is another story! The point is that it was a decision and course of action that needed the impact of one unreasonable individual.

Another, more obvious situation where teams are not appropriate is where the task is so complex that it requires the work of a real expert—a boffin. However, these tasks are rare and even boffins nowadays increasingly depend on teams.

So teams are applicable to most situations. Where they will most often be found is where there is uncertainty; here members can support each other through the difficult periods. Teams are most certainly required where individual tasks are dependent on each other for success of the whole, and where creativity or complex problem-solving are required, the team can often out-perform the individual.

Team *synergy* simply means that the sum contribution of the team exceeds the individual contribution of its members. In other words two plus two *can* equal five!

Implications for the 'new' team leader

If you inherit a team, the autocratic approach is unlikely to be successful for long. It is necessary to become someone who will work *with* the team to achieve joint aims. It is possible to refer to both fact and early literature to show that there has been an innate understanding of this fact for hundreds of years.

TEAM-BUILDING—THE *HENRY V* APPROACH

'We few, we happy few, we band of brothers;
For he today that sheds his blood with me
Shall be my brother; be he ne'er so vile'

Thus spake Harry the King and of course his troops, now remotivated, rallied and despite fearful odds won a famous victory.

Of course, that was the Shakespearean version of events and we do not know whether in real life the king made a motivational, team-building speech before the battle of Agincourt. Nevertheless, the power of the king's speech from *Henry V* echoes down through history. Churchill borrowed elements in his famous speech after the Battle of Britain in which he stated that: 'Never in the field of human conflict, was so much owed by so many to so few.'

After showing the king's speech to managers on leadership programmes, with its common vision, its appeals to group loyalty, and its strong measure of emotion, I have often noted some of the toughest participants surreptitiously reaching for a tissue.

The effective team leader must be someone who can work with the team to agree on and subsequently achieve joint aims. If your aims and those of your team are different, failure is virtually guaranteed and even Henry, the powerful orator, went to great pains to ensure that the team accepted his goals and values.

So let us look at some other vital facts about teams and then go more closely into the behaviours that teams and their members often exhibit. It is through the use of this knowledge that the team leader can build success.

Team behaviour

Teams have been a favourite subject of research for years. Some of the findings, when generalized, may seem blindingly obvious but are, nevertheless, valid and useful to remember.

Key facts

1. The characteristics of teams will differ from team to team, i.e. what worked with one team will not necessarily work with the next.

2. Use different teams for different purposes. Neither individuals nor teams can be 'all things to all men'.

3. When working with teams it is necessary to share information with them. They need it and if they do not have it may rebel faster than a single individual who is kept in the dark.

4. The team will evaluate its leader. It will demand the sort of leadership behaviour it feels is right for it as well as the right level of work.

5. Your behaviour as leader will affect the way that the team behaves and not always in the way you might expect. For example, the extent to which you have defined the roles in the team and its tasks is going to have a profound influence on how members work, how they relate to each other, and how they relate to you.

Some of the most valuable work on teams has been carried out on the issues of how teams develop from scratch into mature performing units and also into the roles that people adopt in teams, with their accompanying behaviour.

The stages of team development

There are generally recognized as being four stages of team development. They are an almost inevitable process and consequently impose certain disciplines on what you, the leader, can do to help the team advance through this process.

The stages of development were first identified by B. W. Tuckman and have been elaborated further by many since then. Attempts have been made to substitute other models but this format has considerable 'face validity' with people who spend much of their time in teams.

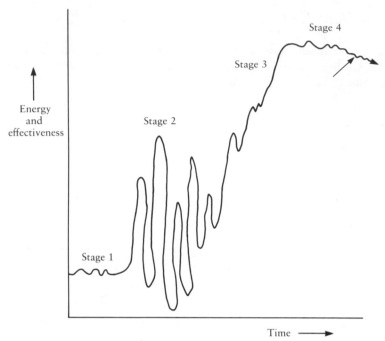

Figure 4.1   The stages of team development.

Stage 1—Forming

The first stage occurs when a new group is brought together. It is not a team yet and the group members may not have worked together before. At this stage they are nervous and watchful. 'What are the others like?' members may think. 'Am I good enough? Until I find out, I am going to keep a low profile.'

So, at this stage there is little energy, and members will be guarded and heavily reliant on the leader to give them a structure for future activity. The clearest example I can think of to illustrate this stage is at the start of a training course. Participants examine each other with unease and often silence reigns supreme. It is clearly up to the programme manager to start the momentum. Figure 4.1 shows that at this stage there is little energy and little effectiveness.

Stage 2—Storming

An interesting stage! Here the members of the team start to confront each other. They may be starting to irritate each other, or they may be feeling frustrated at the team's failure to progress. Some may mentally withdraw while others may challenge the leader. Subgroups may form and these in turn may cause friction.

Remarks that the leader may overhear now may range from 'Why do you always interrupt me? It's getting on my nerves!' to 'This is a waste of time, we're not progressing at all' or 'What are we here for and why don't you contribute, anyway?'

Figure 4.1 shows that this stage is characterized by wild fluctuations of energy and effectiveness. It is, however, a necessary interlude in the development of the team and in itself is healthy. It is a period of sorting out, of clarification of task and roles. Often an unproductive team is recognized as one that has not gone through the storming process.

The role of the leader is to recognize the storm and to steer the team through it. It is only when a team sticks in the storming mode that it is unhealthy and, paradoxically, many team-building exercises are designed to provoke a 'containable' storm where one has not already occurred.

Stage 3—Norming

After the storm comes a period of consolidation and building. Usually because of the storm, clearer roles have been established. Members now are clearer about what is expected of them and are more open with each other and more supportive of each other. This increased openness is probably because there may have been frank or angry exchanges between some members of the team and, human nature being what it is, people whose relationships have gone through traumas are usually more open with each other than those whose relationships have always been placid.

Now you may overhear remarks such as 'We really worked well together on that job!' or 'Well, I couldn't have got there without your help. Now what have we got to do next?'

In terms of Figure 4.1, there is a steady increase over time of effectiveness and effort.

Stage 4—Performing

Here the team has reached a level of settled interdependence. It has tackled a number of tasks successfully in the past and allowances are made for the strengths and weaknesses of its members who are close and supportive. Members work well together and the leader should be able to predict with some degree of certainty how they will tackle problems.

As leader you may simply hear the steady hum of task-related conversations. There is, however, a danger, and one that you ignore at your peril. A team that has reached the performing stage can start to exclude new ideas or new members. It can start to become a clique. When this occurs you are likely to overhear people say 'We're the A Team, who cares what the rest think!' or 'She's not one of us, she doesn't understand what it's like.'

When this occurs, the level of effectiveness begins to drop rather than, as you might expect, stay at a constant high level. A team leader needs to be constantly vigilant for this subtle change. Not surprisingly, it is often when a team is at the performing level that consultants are brought in to run team-building events. Often they create a mini-storm in order to jerk the team from a slow decline up to an even higher level of energy and effectiveness.

Team development—the leader's part

If you lead the team, either as an active member or indirectly, you have a responsibility for its performance. How you lead the group and move it forwards will depend on the way you use your judgement and intuition to help you choose the most suitable behaviour for the situation. However, here are some guidelines to match the four stages:

1. *Forming*   At this stage the team is looking for someone to give it clear goals and to move it in a definitive direction. So, if you do not know what the goals of the team should be then you cannot expect the team to invent them. You need to listen to team members, to provide reassurance and a feeling of belonging for any who may feel excluded, but perhaps, above all, to offer a framework within which the team feels free to operate. Members are probably waiting for direction-giving phrases like: 'This is the way we are going to go about it.' or 'Our first target is . . .'.

2. *Storming*   When a group storms, the leader must decide whether it is best to leave members to work it out for themselves or whether it is best to intervene. If the group does not look as if it is going to learn to work together, then it is best to intervene. Perhaps members' needs are not being met, perhaps differences of opinion or approach are not being resolved—the reasons may be many. Very often a clarification of the roles within the team or of the team's objectives may suffice. If subgroups have formed then rallying words, a touch of *Henry V*, may be what is needed. However, above all, you need to listen and look hard. Your intervention may not be desirable and you may have to do one of the hardest things for a leader to do, that is, stand back and let time and human nature resolve the problem.

3. *Norming*   You may be more relaxed about your team by now. It may not need you to do much but what it may need is a reminder from time to time of its objectives and for you to help it to take on new tasks. Here your role may be much more that of group trainer

than group controller and a reversion to tight control might prove to be very demotivating. The team might still benefit from some motivational words but these words should build on past successes and inspire the team to take on new challenges rather than be heavily directive.

4. *Performing*   The team is doing well at this stage but the pitfalls are either complacency (nobody does it as well as us) or 'group think' (this is the way that we do it here!). So perhaps again you need to look and listen. Can you see some slight falling off of attitude or performance? If so, do you need to give the team some new challenges that may shake the complacency, or do you need to insist that they do a task in a different way?

The chemistry of teams

If there seem to be rather a large number of questions and options open to the leader this is because, as stated earlier, no two teams are the same. Each team is a unique combination of the different personality traits of the people who make it up, so it is quite legitimate to talk of a team having a personality or chemistry.

The most exciting studies of management teams were conducted by Professor Meredith Belbin, who summarized them in his book *Effective Management Teams*. Here Belbin identified eight roles, or preferences of behaviour, that people adopt in teams. There have been other studies since but none, in my opinion, has had the same impact. An endorsement of the validity of Belbin's work comes from the enthusiastic reception it always receives on management courses. People really relate to the roles and recognize large parts of themselves as well as identify the behaviour of their colleagues in them.

It is probably no exaggeration to say that a team leader cannot afford to be be ignorant of these roles, or of the impact that the mixture of them can have on the development of a team.

The team roles are as follows:

1. *The chairman*   This is not a formal position but rather a form of behaviour that some like to adopt. The chairman likes to pull the group together, likes group harmony and for the group to be focused, and will consequently act in a similar fashion to the classical chairman's role. These people will coordinate activities, will try and make sure that everybody has their say and will listen well, will work through other people by assigning tasks, and will

generally help to move the group forwards in a steady, harmonious, and focused way. They may not always make a creative contribution themselves but they can bring out creativity in others.

2. *The shaper*   This person is very different. Shapers are impatient drivers who are extremely task orientated and who can exude nervous energy. They can be abrasive and 'pushy'. They can upset others and they can sulk when they do not get their own way. They may not always be easy to have around but they are necessary as they can move a team forwards through the stages. They also make sure that objectives are met, even if it tends to be the way that the shaper thinks it should be done. George Bernard Shaw said, 'all progress depends on the unreasonable man'.

Shapers can help move a team towards its goals and can be especially useful in a crisis situation.

3. *The plant*   Not a vegetable but an ideas person. However, like a real plant, this team member needs to be nurtured. The plant is intellectually dominant but introverted. Plants may think of good ideas that will benefit the team but if another team member criticizes that idea, they may feel hurt and no longer contribute, thinking thoughts like: 'Why should I cast my pearls before swine?'

It is up to the good leader to recognize plants and to give them the opportunity to be heard by drawing them out and praising their contribution. If you do not do this your team may be the poorer as a result.

4. *The monitor evaluator*   This person will be analytical and intelligent, and may also appear cold and aloof. When ideas are mooted, monitor evaluators will analyse them and then pass candid and sometimes tactless comment. They do not suffer fools gladly! They are very useful in ensuring that the team does not waste its time on scatterbrained ideas or go off on a wild goose chase, but by being tactless they can at times restrict group creativity.

If you think you have a monitor evaluator in your group then be careful to allow that person just enough scope to be a benefit to, rather than a destructive force within, the team.

5. *The company worker*   This team member is sometimes called 'the implementer'. Implementers get things done, they are good at charting and scheduling activities and will make sure that plans are turned into reality. They are usually reliable although may not contribute to the creativity of the group. The company worker's name, however, is the one most likely to be found against the 'actions' in the minutes of a meeting.

If you want to be sure that things will be achieved and that the team is more than just a 'talking shop', then you should try to ensure that you have a company worker in it.

6. *The team worker*   This person gets pleasure simply from being in a team. Team workers are sociable, uncompetitive, and try to promote group harmony. They will not compete for leadership but will try to bind the group together by supportive behaviour. The team worker's main contribution is essentially a unifying one and if that does not seem important, then think of any successful sports team: for every star player there are any number of supporting players without whose efforts the star would not be able to shine.

7. *The resource investigator*   A member who gets pleasure from looking outside the team, making contacts and then bringing new ideas or information into the team as a result of those efforts. Resource investigators are, as you may imagine, sociable and friendly. They always know someone who has the information that the team needs. They are often on the telephone or out to lunch and as such are useful to the team, although they do have a tendency to be casual. Their main pleasure comes from making and pursuing their contacts rather than from giving accurate and timely information.

   For teams that are geared towards the achievement of some tasks, resource investigators are vital; they do, however, need to be controlled.

8. *The completer finisher*   Finishers are just that. They will remind the group of deadlines and targets and relentlessly follow them through. Completer finishers will nag and chivvy other team members if they think they are lagging behind targets, and consequently they are not always popular with others. However, when the team is working on jobs with clear deadlines their contribution is imperative.

Knowledge and use of team roles

The interesting thing about the team roles is that we all will have the attributes of the majority of them within our personalities to a greater or lesser extent. Some characteristics will prevail over others and so you may already be relating to some of these descriptions more than to others.

Belbin argued that a good team will contain a wide spread of the roles and that they will then become part of the strength of the team. I would agree with that and advise a team leader to get the team to complete the team roles questionnaire. This will indicate the spread of talents, or chemistry, of the team and also give a good basis for non-personal feedback in any subsequent team-building event, i.e. the behaviour can be criticized in terms of the team role displayed, rather than the person.

The effective team

Setting the team roles aside for a moment, what does a really good team look like and how can the leader get it there? While no two teams will be identical, there are several indicators that will show that a team is effective. Here then are some signs that a team has reached, and is maintaining, the 'Performing' level:

- Team members support each other in achieving both individual and group tasks.

- Progress towards targets is reviewed regularly and then new plans are made without prompting from the leader.

- Members communicate well with each other. There is trust and respect as well as candid feedback.

- The team generates its own energy. There is probably a high level of humour in the way that members interact.

- Members enjoy meeting as a group yet also see the need to communicate positively with other groups and individuals. The team is aware of the dangers of becoming a clique.

- Team members inform you of the type of leadership they would most value from you.

If you have a team that shows all of these characteristics then you are indeed fortunate. However, usually we make our own luck; here are some ways by which you can steer the team towards optimum performance.

Steering your team

1. *Build trust*   Trust must flow in all directions. It must exist between the leader and the team as well as between individual team members. One way to do this is to stamp out any internal politics or unproductive in-fighting. In doing this you should make it clear that this is simply not acceptable behaviour. At the same time it is important not to become embroiled yourself in the politics of the team. Be above it and stamp on it!

In saying this I am not recommending political naivety, far from it. Organizational politics exist and you may have to 'play' to an extent. However, never play politics with your own team, the boomerang effect will inevitably follow.

2. *Choose the team wisely*   Although most leaders in business will inherit the team, there will be times when it expands or when members change that will give you the opportunity of selecting new members. When you have this opportunity think carefully about the roles that you have already observed within the team. Is a vital role missing, or do you already have too many people who adopt some other role? You may be thinking: 'What we really need is a resource investigator for this group.' or 'We cannot afford another shaper. There is enough arguing already!'

3. *Be accepting*   When you see interdependence among team members accept it, even if it means that they are not approaching you for advice so often. If they are helping each other, that in itself is a good thing.

4. *Reinforce goals and values*   Members of an effective team should have the same goals, i.e. 'What are we here to achieve?' and the same values, i.e. 'How do we go about achieving these goals?' They will have formed common views as to what is and is not acceptable behaviour. If you see differences of opinion in these important areas, you may wish to take a more upfront role by calling a meeting to address the differences or by setting up a team-building event with those issues placed firmly on the agenda.

5. *Adjust your behaviour as leader*   Remember that teams at different stages of development will respond to different types of approach. Once again *flexibility* is a key word and you will have to exercise choice.

Just what sort of choices you have and why you will need to exercise them can be seen by looking further at the future of teams, of the leader's role in them and of the implications of these developments for both teams and their leaders.

The trend towards the self-managing team

A number of studies have shown that it is in the direction of the *self-managing team* that modern teams in forward-looking organizations are moving. But what is it and is it as big a threat to the leader as the term suggests?

The self-managing, or bossless, team is becoming increasingly common in the workplace, and all indications are that it is here to stay. It has come into existence both through changes in the way that organizations work, as seen in moves towards project teams, brand management teams, installation teams, and task forces, as well as through changes to the very structure of organizations themselves, as covered earlier in this chapter.

Needless to say, the self-managing team has attracted a good deal of curiosity among both academics and practicing managers. The questions that always arise are:

- What is now the role of the manager?
- What sort of behaviour should be adopted and how can any form of leadership be displayed without it appearing to be a contradiction in terms?

In trying to answer these questions the advice for the team leader is that one of the hardest forms of behaviour must be adopted. The leader must learn that by letting go, and by allowing the team to function increasingly without overt control, both power and authority will be maintained and may in fact, even grow. Fight against the trend and you will do yourself no favours!

The team leader versus the solo leader

In his article 'Solo leader/team leader: antithesis in style and structure', Meredith Belbin contrasts two different styles of team leadership. He states that one form of team leadership is that of the *solo leader*.

The solo leader plays an unlimited role within the team (interferes?), strives for conformity of approach from team members and collects acolytes. Subordinates are constantly directed and the leader's personal objectives are projected onto the team. Belbin suggests that this was the style of leadership that Margeret Thatcher imposed on the cabinet before she was deposed, and that it is inappropriate for a mature and skilful team.

The alternative is to be a *team leader*. Skilful team leaders choose to limit their roles, i.e. they delegate authority and seek to develop talent from within the team. If there is diversity of opinion within the team they try to build on the diversity by encouraging members to value their differences. They develop talents from within the team and create a sense of mission which the team also feels that it owns.

The team leader as broker

Zenger, Mussewhite, Hurson, and Perrin go one stage further. They state that: 'The well documented vitality of teams in no way devalues the need

A	B	C
When used alone, these skills are suited only to a rigidly traditional workplace	*With column A skills, these are needed in today's more progressive workplace*	*With column A and B skills, these are needed to build and maintain a team environment*
Direct people.	Involve people.	Develop self-motivated people who set their own goals and evaluate their own efforts.
Get people to understand ideas.	Get people to generate ideas.	Get groups of diverse people to generate and implement their own best ideas.
Manage one-on-one.	Encourage teamwork.	Build teams that manage more of their own day-to-day work.
Maximize the department's performance.	Build relationships with other departments.	Champion cross-functional efforts to improve quality, service, and productivity.
Implement changes imposed from above.	Initiate changes within the department.	Anticipate, initiate, and respond to changes dictated by forces outside the organization.

By permission Zenger, Musselwhite, Zenger and Perrin

Figure 4.2   Three skill layers for managers.

for skilled managers. What's called for now is a different kind of manager—more strategic, more collaborative, more facilitative and more responsive to customers, employees and organizational imperatives.' and also say that 'Today's manager builds team members' skills and confidence, gradually delegates new tasks and helps employees set goals . . .'. This is quite a challenge and their table of three skill levels for managers (Figure 4.2), shows that the leader who is able to operate effectively in this sort of environment, and especially in the ways implicit within column three, will be a far more sophisticated leader than Belbin's solo leader. This person will be both leader and broker of power and information.

The concept of leader as broker is enlarged on in an interesting article by David Barry in which he states that there is a trend towards distributed leadership within bossless teams. In other words, more than one person may play a leading role in a team in order to meet different needs. Consequently the leadership is *not person centered but role centred*.

Barry states that the leadership roles and behaviours required for proper self-managing team (SMT) functioning fall into four broad clusters:

1. *Envisioning*   The task of creating a new and exciting vision for the team and facilitating the generation of ideas and goals.

2. *Organizing*   People who adopt this role get the group to focus on details, structure, and deadlines. They are good at making things predictable and clear.

3. *Spanning*   This form of leadership involves linking the team's efforts with other groups and individuals. People who like to adopt this role will be good networkers, and by making external links will provide the team with a constant source of reality checks.

4. *Social leadership*   This involves developing the group as a social entity, by mediating where there are conflicts and ensuring that members collaborate with each other. Belbin's chairman would be good in this form of leadership.

Any of these forms of leadership may be appropriate for particular tasks that face the team. Remember, these are roles that are adopted by team members, not by the formal leader.

The 'formal' leader's role is to ensure that these other forms of leadership emerge in other people and are used at the right time. Once again, this is not an easy role, but a facilitative role rather than use of behaviour in the mould of a Henry V. But is there any place today for Henry? After all he was very effective once and he was absolutely inspiring to his followers. Perhaps the answer to all you frustrated Henrys (whether you be male or female Henrys) lies in the *visionary team leader*.

The visionary team leader

The concept of the visionary team leader (VTL) was created by Rupert Eales-White in *The Power of Persuasion*. This leader is essentially group oriented and has strong visionary skills. At the same time the VTL is a good listener and believes in both motivating and empowering team members. So the VTL has all the talents of Henry but chooses wisely how and when to use them. The VTL is a visionary change agent but acts for and with the team rather than in a selfish ego-centred way.

Once again it comes down to a matter of choice. With delayering, people in teams are likely to be more demanding as well as more independent. They will be looking for a variety of behaviours from the leader. Sometimes they may want their leader to be virtually invisible, and just occasionally they may seek inspiration. The VTL accurately judges what is required and responds with flexibility.

The team-building event (or what to do when a team is not performing)

Some teams seem to work effectively right from the start, while others never seem to get going. The team building event is a means of getting the most out of your team, whether you are Henry V, the VTL, or even the solo leader. However, if you are a solo leader you are likely to find the whole process somewhat threatening!

So, why run a team-building event in the first place? Sometimes team-building events are run because everything appears to be going well. The golfing weekend at which two hours at the end of the day is devoted to discussing business issues is one form of team-building event, as is the departmental Christmas Dinner at which people get tipsy and feel free to say what they really feel about certain issues (and spend the whole of the following day regretting their indiscretions).

However, real team-building is run for a purpose. There may be a number of issues that prompt such an event and these may be any of the following:

- Team considers it has unclear goals or objectives.
- Productivity is lower than expected.
- Morale is low in the team.
- There is confusion about individual roles or responsibilities.
- The leader detects hostility from the team.

When the need for team building has been identified two further issues arise. Can we do this ourselves? What form should it take?

The first question is fundamental. Although you may be tempted to show creative leadership by setting up and running the event yourself, beware, there are pitfalls. First, people may not open up, which is a problem, and secondly, they may open up too much, which can be a greater problem if you do not know how to handle the group dynamics.

A suggested 'safe' route for a self-run team-build would be for all members of the team to complete the Belbin questionnaire and then compare their behaviour preferences with a view to discussing the following question: 'How can we work better as a team, bearing in mind the different strengths we bring to it?'

Other approaches to team-building are less safe and may well require an external facilitator to aid proceedings. To give an example of why an external facilitator is useful, here are some of the questions that person may ask at the start of the process. All of the questions are very simple but please note—they can be dynamite!

- Do we really need to collaborate?

- Do we really want change?

- Is the leader really committed to this or are we playing games?

- Are we willing to keep an open mind during the event?

- Are people prepared to be both honest and critical?

IGNORING THE QUESTIONS—AN EXAMPLE

I once ran a team-building day for a small advertising agency. Its CEO was also its founder and was a powerful entrepreneur. Before the event, he told me that he wished that his co-directors would challenge him more often. At the start of the event we went through the questions listed above and everybody nodded.

During the morning the team embarked on a difficult exercise and the CEO began to assert his will until there was an explosion from the most junior member of the board. 'You always do this to us! You start us off on a project and then you override us, it's always done *your* way. Have you any idea how that demotivates us?'

The CEO went very red and for a moment I thought that I was going to be sent packing. Then he looked at the questions that he had agreed to and with an amused shrug looked back at his criticizer. 'You are quite right,' he said, 'and what are we here for, anyway?'

After this explosion it was quite easy to refer the team to the stages of team development, find out where they thought they were at that moment, and then to obtain commitments as to what they all felt they should do to move the team ahead.

Variations on team-building

Team-building events can take a number of different forms. Some concentrate on joint problem-solving and then examine what went on between members as they tackled the problem. The lessons from the simulated problem are usually quickly related to what goes on in real life.

Other events are more emotionally taxing. One exercise that can really sort out relationships is based on a candid exchange of 'wants' and 'offers' between members. People get together in pairs and tell each other 'What I want from you that I am not getting at present', i.e. listen to me for a change, and then 'What I am able to offer you that may help our working relationship'.

It requires little imagination to see that such events do need skilful facilitation. However, those that do work can greatly help the team as well as help its leader to move towards becoming a VTL.

Reasons why team-building can fail

If this section on team-building seems to be full of caveats, it is because the process can go wrong if not correctly handled. On the other hand, the benefits of a well-run event are enormous. Leaders in the future will increasingly be working through teams and devolving more of their authority to them. Consequently, I would like to end this chapter with a few words on why team-building events may not produce the expected results. Reasons may be complex and many, but here are some of the more obvious ones:

- Team-building is seen as a short-term answer to all ills. (It isn't. Teams require on-going maintenance.)

- Nobody does anything after the event and credibility is lost.

- Members have the misconception that they should all be deliriously happy after the event. (This need not be the case and could be a sign that issues have been fudged.)

Summary

So, leading a team as well as running a team-building event are both serious business. Teams, however, are both the model of future work patterns and a continual challenge to leaders in their choice of approach. Teams, as well as individuals, have to be motivated—the same rules apply. How well a team is motivated depends on how aware the leader is of the roles as well as the processes at work in it. The new leader, however, does have access to a number of vehicles for a better understanding of the team and for helping it to move forwards successfully. It is up to that leader to use those vehicles!

Your WIFMs from this chapter

- What is the current status of teams within your organization and what is the consequent challenge to you as a leader?

- Do you constantly look for ways of achieving synergy from your team? If it is not present why is that the case?

- How can you best work *with* your team rather than simply have it work *for* you?

- At what stage of development is your team? What might you need to do to move it forwards?

- Have you analysed your own preferred team roles and those of your team members? How might the varying strengths best be balanced to bring about a more effective team?

- Are you part of a self-managing team or do you have a team working for you that could become self-managing? Can you encourage this to happen and what are the implications for your own role?

- What do you personally need to do to become a VTL?

- Would you and your team benefit from a team-building event? How will you ensure that it succeeds?

The leader as motivator and persuader

Very early in my career I used to catch a commuter train to London from Sevenoaks in Kent. The train was always crowded, and by the time it reached Sevenoaks all the seats were taken. Being a creature of habit I always used to get into the same carriage and stand looking down on the passengers who were lucky enough to have seats. One couple always amused me. They were fast asleep when I boarded the train and still fast asleep when I disembarked at the penultimate stop. The man had a black goatee beard and the woman had brown swept back hair. They used to sleep with their heads on each other's shoulders and in over a year, I never saw them awake.

Eighteen years passed and circumstances meant that I was forced to take an early train from Sevenoaks to London after a long gap. To my amazement, I found myself looking down on the same couple. They were both still fast asleep but the years had wrought their changes. The man's beard had turned white and the woman's hair was now streaked with grey, and she wore granny spectacles balanced on the end of her nose.

Apart from fantasizing that they had never got off the train and that they had been carried, Rip Van Winkle-like backwards and forwards over the years, I was compelled to wonder what it was that had kept them going, that had motivated them over the years as their lives had slowly ticked away. Was it grim necessity? Or did they love their work? What did they think of their respective bosses? And to what extent had those leaders played a part in making those intervening years a pleasure, or miserable? On the other hand, would the following telling words from Bill O'Brien of Hanover Insurance be applicable to them?

'People enter business as bright, well educated, high energy people with a desire to make a difference. By the time they are thirty, a few are on the "fast track" and the rest "put in their time" to do what matters to them at the weekend. They lose their commitment, the sense of mission and the excitement with which they started their career. We get damn little of their energy and almost none of their spirit'

I never knew the answer to my questions, but one thing I am sure of is that those people who led them would have had a greater impact on the quality of their lives than they would ever have imagined, and in many respects those words identify both the problem as well as the challenge for leaders at all levels of business today. But first, some thoughts to back these words.

The motivation to work—theory X or theory Y?

If we make the somewhat naive assumption that it is better if people enjoy the time they spend at work and fill those hours with their greatest energy and creativity, then perhaps a good place to start in examining the subjects of motivation and persuasion is by asking: 'Why do people work?'
     Here are some of the answers.

For money	For companionship
Security	Achievement
To escape boredom	For interest/challenge
Conditioning	Status
Social acceptability	To help others

Read the two columns. Which of the reasons do you feel are the more compelling, those on the left (column 1) or on the right (column 2)? If you consider that the answers in column 1 are the more important you are probably what D. McGregor would call a theory X manager and if you consider that the answers in column 2 are the most important then you may be what he would call a theory Y manager.
     The difference between theory X and theory Y managers is simple. The theory X manager believes that people are born lazy and that given half a chance, they will avoid work or do the minimum they can get away with. Consequently, they must be closely supervised and coerced into working via direct orders and threats.
     The theory Y manager, on the other hand, believes that people love to work and will seek work out as a means of self-expression and fulfilment. The theory Y manager will point to great achievements, both scientific and artistic, to back this claim. Therefore, says the theory Y manager, create the right environment, motivate your people correctly, and they will repay you through hard and dedicated labour.
     I take an optimistic view of the human condition and so place myself firmly in the Y camp. But what is motivation and how does the leader motivate others to generate excellent business results?

The essence of motivation

A great deal has been written about motivation, theoretically and in practical terms. The basic concept, however, is quite simple. Healthy people have energy, they also have the ability to think creative thoughts, solve problems, and to work hard in doing so. However, for much of the time this energy remains locked up, the individual chooses *not* to give it to an employer.

At the same time, this person may give a great deal of energy to other non-work-related activities—so the energy does exist. The challenge to you as leader is that of unlocking the energy of others, of making them *want* to give you all the energy, effort, and ingenuity that they so often give to other non-work-related activities.

The leader who finds the key to unlock these talents has found one of the keys to long-term effective leadership. It is all too easy to state blandly that money is the sole key to the release of energy, as the following case illustrates.

A MOTIVATED HIGH ACHIEVER

When working for Rank Xerox, I visited one of their northern offices in the mid seventies. A salesman was pointed out to me with something close to reverence. This man had made one of the biggest sales in the history of the branch. This meant that in one month alone he had earned £7000 in commission above his basic salary. Furthermore, he had qualified as one of the top 20 salespeople of the year and had therefore won a holiday overseas. If that were not enough, the company had been running a special incentive competition for the top sale that month, which he had won. The prize was an MG sports car. Little wonder he was highly motivated and in high spirits—especially as in that month alone his commission had totalled over twice the national average wage. It would be easy to say that he was motivated by money alone, but years later when Rank Xerox was no longer enjoying the massive profits that allowed them to pay in this way I was told that he still worked as hard and with the same cheerful enthusiasm although his earnings were now well down. So what was it that kept him motivated? What were the keys?

In searching for the keys, it will be necessary to look at elements of the theory of motivation as well as the strictly practical ways in which people can be motivated and persuaded.

Motivation—the theory

In looking at the theory of motivation, it is always necessary to approach it in the most pragmatic fashion—what is in it for you? The subject of motivation is one in which the theorists have had a field day and it remains one of great interest and much research. After all, the person who fully identifies how to release the energy of other people has found the behavioural equivalent of the Holy Grail.

Research still continues on the subject and it would be easy to fill an entire book with it. Without apology, however, I will concentrate on some of the early, better known work before going on to develop other thoughts and themes. The reasons for doing so are simple. First of all, much of what has followed is based on these early premises. Secondly, an idea is not devalued simply because it has been around for a long time (if that were the case, all religion and most classical music and literature would be worthless). Finally, the early theorists relate most easily to the vital question of how we can get others to give us their energy and commitment. Much of the theory can be reduced to the simple statement that:

NEEDS create BEHAVIOUR that satisfies GOALS

If you really want something, you will act in such a way as to obtain it. If you are hungry you will buy food and the food will satisfy your immediate goal of having a full stomach. So, identify the other person's needs correctly and you can either predict with some accuracy how they will behave or identify what you need to do to help them satisfy their goals and in doing so also release their energy to help you.

This process involves the identification of the other person's WIFMs so put yourself into the other person's shoes—what are their WIFMs? If you can identify the other person's WIFMs then you will have the key to motivating them.

But how are WIFMs identified? Academic theory holds many of the answers, and having looked at some of the concepts involved in the theory it will then be necessary to examine strategies for making them work for you.

Early theorists: Maslow and Herzberg

Maslow

Maslow is probably the best known of the early theorists. He wanted to show how people's needs govern their behaviour and how actions can be explained in terms of individuals trying to satisfy those needs.

Maslow proposed that humans have five categories of needs and that they are ordered hierarchically. In other words, until one need is met, the individual will not expend energy on meeting other needs.

Once a need has been met, or satisfied, it will not stimulate the individual into a particular course of action until it is threatened. It may then return with a vengeance.

Maslow ranked the needs as follows:

1. *Physiological*   This is the basic need to keep the body alive. We need food, water, shelter, and sleep. In the world of work we do not find many people operating at this level.

2. *Security*   This can be seen as the need for a secure job, the knowledge that it will be there tomorrow, and the knowledge that the employer will provide some cushion of benefits if things go wrong.

3. *Social*   Human beings are social animals. In the working environment this need is as pronounced as anywhere. We all want a sense of identity and the comfort of being accepted by the group; after all, if we are not accepted, if the group does not feel that we will make a valuable contribution to it, we may not be allowed to remain in it.

4. *Esteem*   Most of us need a sense of self-esteem. In the workplace this ties in with a need for recognition of our achievements, to be known to be good at what we do, and to have chances of further advancement and status within the organization. If we are worried about our security or general acceptance we are unlikely to be motivated by this need.

5. *Self-fulfilment*   Maslow places this need at the top of his hierarchy. At this stage individuals place emphasis on the full use of all their abilities, they seek full self-expression and want to be themselves in the fullest way possible. It is not that people who are worried about their security or who are wondering where their next meal is coming from have no wish to make the most of their full potential, simply that for the time being, it is a long way down their list of priorities.

The key message

The essential message behind Maslow's theory is that the hierarchy represents a path along which people develop. The further along it they move, the more in control of their destiny they will feel and the more proactive in approach they will become. So, the short message is: *do everything you can to make your staff feel recognized and that their abilities are being used. They will repay you tenfold!*

But people can move up and down the hierarchy quite quickly. Take the following scenario, for example.

THE SURVIVORS

One of the most dramatic examples of people being forced rapidly through the Maslow hierarchy can be seen in the case of the Andes survivors. Here, a number of wealthy young Uruguayans were involved in a drastic air disaster in the middle of the Andes range of mountains. Many of the passengers were killed but a number survived unscathed, including members of a rugby team and their friends.

The conditions were freezing and food supplies virtually non-existent. Within days the survivors were reduced to cannibalism and this kept them alive for several weeks until some eventually were able to summon help. From level 5 they were rapidly reduced to level 1 and even after their rescue, it took them a long time to return to level 3 owing to extreme feelings of shame and some public censure. It is one thing to act in desperation and quite another thing to believe that your actions are condoned when you are back in a normal situation again.

What is the lesson from this? Maslow has been challenged by revisionists but his theory is relevant. People feel the needs quite strongly and the theory has a degree of universality. Although some cultures' definitions of self-fulfilment may differ, the basic principles remain. Even the South Sea Islanders living in their so-called tropical paradises feel the pain of being at level 1, as Lucy Irvine found out to her cost.

Take time to think about where your people may be on the hierarchy of needs. Their position will dictate their WIFMs and your behaviour as leader will have a major influence on where they end up on the continuum. The leader who has most staff at the higher levels is most likely to have a team that is able to tackle complex tasks with enthusiasm and the minimum supervision.

With WIFMs in mind, another theorist who had considerable influence and who is seen as placing Maslow's hierarchy into a work setting was Herzberg.

Herzberg

Herzberg asked a large number of working people to recall both the high spots and the low spots of their working lives and to state what it was that made the good times good and the bad times bad. Some interesting findings emerged.

When people felt worst about their jobs it was often because there was something wrong with one of the following factors:

- Status

- Security

- Work conditions

- Relationship with others
- Salary
- Swamped by bureaucracy
- Relationship with boss

When they had felt really good about their jobs it was often to do with:

- Being able to achieve things
- Being recognized
- Being given responsibility
- Growing and learning in the job
- The work itself being interesting
- Ability for advancement

The periods of dissatisfaction were largely accounted for by events related to the context of the job. If the company gets these areas right then, said Herzberg, people will experience an absence of dissatisfaction. He therefore called them *hygiene factors* because they performed a preventative function.

In contrast, the periods of satisfaction usually related to the content of the job. If they were there they tended to create job satisfaction. Herzberg stated that if these factors, which he called *motivators*, were not present it would not lead to job dissatisfaction although, as we are generally more demanding of the quality of our lives nowadays, I consider that statement to be increasingly questionable.

Although the research on which Herzberg based his theory is old, I have noticed that people at work and the many that I meet on management training programmes still relate strongly to the words, concepts, and emotions implicit in the theory.

Two interesting facts about the theory of hygiene factors and motivators are:

1. Motivators usually work more powerfully than hygiene factors.

2. The leader, even if not CEO, can usually do more to influence motivators than hygiene factors.

Just think of it. What can most managers do to change working conditions or company policy? Probably not much. However, you can probably do a great deal to make people's work more interesting, to make them feel that they are getting somewhere, and that what they are doing is being recognized. Motivators are often linked to your staff's individual WIFMs, and you often need only to put yourself into their shoes to make a major difference to the amount of energy they are going to give you.

A procedure for bringing about this release of energy was devised by E. Lawler.

Lawler—a more recent approach

While both the Maslow and Herzberg models are good general theories, it is the model of motivation devised by Lawler that can be most easily used as a workable procedure by individual managers. This is a procedure that can be used both to further motivate the motivated and to diagnose problem areas where people are unmotivated.

The common sense of motivation

Lawler stated that the expenditure of effort should lead to performance, but then asked what it would take to bring about this effort, i.e. make people give their energy to you. He said that there were two prerequisites:

- They should know what to do, and
- They should know how to do it.

If you think that this is simply common sense, it is worth wondering how many people have been demotivated in the past by their boss's assuming they knew how to do things and then having blamed them when things have gone wrong.

The next step is that the necessary resources to do the work should be made available to them. Once again, how many projects have failed because the boss has not provided the right resources for it to succeed in the form of budgets, staffing levels, etc., and has not listened when the subordinate has challenged by saying: 'Do you seriously expect me to do it on *that* budget?'

So, given these prerequisites, the individual should not only start to perform, knowing that their performance will generate rewards for them, but also be further motivated to perform by realizing that the rewards that they will receive are of value to them.

The rewards that they see as coming from their efforts should also be seen as fair and equitable by them. Once again the WIFM concept arises. If the rewards, whether they are in the form of money, bonus, or any other measure, are not seen to be fair in comparison with the effort expended in achieving them, then people will start to lose interest or become resentful. So once again ask: what may be of value to the staff? Is it money, security, a sense of achievement? And can I offer that as a valued reward if targets are met?

Linking Lawler and Herzberg

False assumptions are often made about what is likely to motivate people as rewards. In his article 'The lessons of motivation', Chris Emmins says that many motivational reward schemes, which offer what are essentially bribes in the form of gifts or travel for high individual performance, are not genuinely motivational and are often merely the cause of jealousy among those who have not received these rewards.

I heard one true horror story of a telesales firm that offered a holiday in the Bahamas for its leading salesperson. The sting in the tail was that all the other salespeople were required to go to the airport in their own time in order to see the winner off!

This philosophy contrasts directly with the approach recommended by David Drennan in *Transforming Company Culture*. Although overtly about culture, this book has a major subtheme of practical motivation. Drennan pushes the power of visible recognition of success and status and states that the signs need not be costly but merely statements that the individual's contribution has been valued—he cites the motivational power of medals to soldiers.

More important, he concedes, is the need to make the whole company feel like heroes. Can achievements like the award of a BSI Total Quality Award be the cause of celebration and public team recognition, he asks. Every survey (says Emmins) conducted into motivation yields that employees want the same things:

- They want to be proud of their company.

- They want to do their best.

- They want to learn.

- They want recognition and respect.

- They want to enjoy work.

Emmins' thoughts are clearly backed by Drennan who states that it is the 'fundamental and cherished things' like feeling respected, feeling needed, feeling you belong, feeling somebody cares, that will bring about the behaviour you wish to see. It is surprising (or is it?) how closely this links back to Maslow, Herzberg, and Lawler. When I was a student in Leeds, somebody had written a particular piece of graffiti on a wall there. Other pieces of graffiti came and went, but this one stayed. It read, 'People not personnel!' How true!

The links with Herzberg's motivators are clear. Often the simpler (and cheaper) rewards are the strongest motivators. Lawler mentions feedback as a necessary part of his motivational process and this cheap commodity is so often overlooked. People both want and need feedback. How often do we hear the question: 'How am I doing?'

Feedback can take the form of individual feedback on someone's performance on a negotiation, or can take the form of group feedback on a team's efforts and the subsequent effect on sales or production. In all events it is vital. Without it, people work in the dark and those who try to advance in obscurity are known to stumble and lose confidence. If they do try again it is often with reduced effort and considerable misgivings.

Some practical lessons

So, what can be taken from the theorists and translated into definable tasks that can easily be enacted?

People want to feel valued and will repay this. Make them feel valued by:

1. Regularly monitoring their work and giving specific feedback.

2. Listening to their ideas.

3. Listening to their concerns.

4. Ensuring that everybody understands the value of their contribution to the team goals.

5. Making sure that the function of the organization is understood and that rules and regulations are fully explained.

People want to feel that they are growing and developing in their jobs. Help them develop by:

1. Setting achievable but stretching targets.

2. Providing the training that will help them meet those targets.

3. Allowing people to train one another, thereby developing a whole new set of skills.

4. Looking at jobs under your control to see whether they can be made more interesting and more challenging.

5. Involving them in problem-solving and showing them that you trust and respect their opinions.

When people achieve, or meet targets, recognize this by:

1. Praising them. We so often take effort for granted and forget this vital step.
2. Tell them how their achievements have contributed to the overall success of the company or department.

People rise to challenges. Provide them by:

1. Communicating the team's objectives and by holding members accountable.
2. Giving individuals responsibility (ownership) for particular tasks or functions.
3. Giving people autonomy. Let them do it their way, they will identify more with the outcomes.
4. Encouraging ideas and then giving people the responsibility for implementing them.

Motivating when morale is low

Of course all of this presupposes that morale is at a reasonable level and that most staff are ready, if not eager, to be further motivated. There may be times, however, when morale is very low and theory must take second place to action. If you inherit, or even have caused, a climate of low morale a number of steps will be necessary before more conventional motivators become applicable.

The most important step is to identify what is causing the problem. Is it an individual or a situation? To find out you will have to do a lot of listening, and will also need to ask very searching questions. When listening, seek to understand, not to blame. Blame (if appropriate) comes later.

When you feel that you understand the issues and have a finger on the pulse of the emotions within the group, share your concerns with team members, and give your open support to those who want to put things right, but allow time for those who need more in order to come round.

It may be necessary to set new targets and objectives for both the team and individuals. Again, make sure that these targets are realistic. One way of doing this would be to hold a team building event at which a number of issues can be raised, not least the expectations that the group holds of its leader.

A team-based facilitative approach to motivation

Many of the theories of motivation work well at the individual level but tend to lose applicability when applied at a team or organizational level. At a time when team-based approaches are coming more to the fore, it is therefore appropriate to look at ways in which the leader can act to release the team's energy. The method I have devised applies a situational approach to team motivation and involves the leader in first assessing the essential needs of the group or team and then in selecting the most appropriate approach to facilitating its learning and development. At this stage, therefore, it is necessary to define the concept of 'facilitation'.

Facilitation is allied to coaching but is different. To facilitate is to assist the process of something, to encourage a positive outcome. What distinguishes it from coaching is that it is most often done with groups of people on team-building events or the more sophisticated training programmes where participants are encouraged to take responsibility for their own learning. The quality of the facilitation is evident in the way that the 'leader' chooses to work with the group. This could involve all or more of the following activities:

- Asking questions that help the group reach the right answer.
- Providing answers that unlock understanding, having made the group think along the way.
- Listening to the group's needs, concerns and mood—then reacting appropriately.
- Adapting to the group but having the authority to make it adapt to you when necessary.

These activities can be formalized into four main approaches (Figure 5.1), each of which makes different demands on the leader and assumes different group needs.

1 Intellectual command

This approach is characterized by a high degree of input of data, opinion, and information to the group, but a comparatively low level of intervention into the way that the group members interact with each other (the process). The leader's behaviour should involve guiding by having clear opinions, provoking and answering questions, setting challenges for the group and inputting facts and knowledge where deemed necessary. Intellectual command is appropriate where the team has clear, task-related objectives yet may lack specialist knowledge or information. This may be hindering progress and members may be hungry for knowledge, or direc-

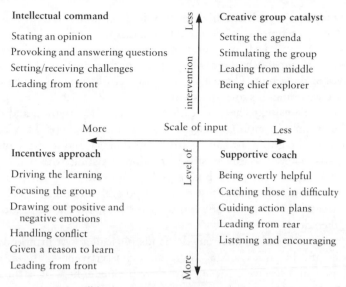

Figure 5.1   ICIS facilitation model.

tion. In the past, the group may have become used to being told the 'right way' by a guru-style leader, yet at the same time members may be intellectually arrogant and prone to overintellectualization. The group have a lot of potential energy but need the challenge of informed and structured questions to release this energy.

This approach makes a number of requirements of the leader, who must be able to display an authoritative understanding of the subject matter or the objectives that the group is addressing. Leaders working in this mode must retain a clear mind and objectivity at all times, have clear opinions and the confidence to state them, and have the flexibility to address the problem from a number of different angles. This will enable them to phrase demanding questions and to 'wow' team members with their demonstrable insight.

Although, this is primarily an upfront, knowledge-input, leading-from-the-front role, the leader must retain the common sense to know when to step back and know when to stop dominating and allow the team to start working out solutions for itself.

2   Incentives approach

This approach is characterized by a high level of input to the knowledge base of the team as well as a high level of intervention in the process of the group. Groups requiring this approach to motivate them may be character-ized by an overall lack of energy or commitment, observable cynicism from some members, and possible open conflict against the tasks and objectives of the group. There may be a number of 'Why are we here?' and 'What are we doing this for?' questions.

It is the responsibility here of leaders to assess the situation and then to drive the group to a more productive state and atmosphere. They must be able to focus the group, to handle any overt conflict and to draw out both the negative as well as the positive emotions existing within the group. Fact and opinion are stated but, equally important, the process of the group is actively influenced by strong and possibly courageous behaviour. If it is necessary to use the stick and carrot to stress the implications of failure, then do so.

This approach makes different demands on leaders—a firm knowledge base is helpful but not enough. High energy, assertiveness, and an ability to both give and receive criticism are all reqirements here. It is the energy and firmness illustrated in this approach that will kick-start the group. The motivation may not be immediate but later, when motivation is higher, members may look back on that intervention as a turning point.

3   Creative group catalyst

This approach is illustrated by less intervention in the group process and a low input of facts and opinions. Teams benefiting from this approach will have a desire to solve their own problems and have a high opinion of their own ability. They may, however, need some steering towards achieving their objectives and may need to be challenged in order to release further energy.

The leader's role here is hard for some as it involves the stimulation of the group but not in an overt way. Actions may involve helping members to set the agenda, giving occasional feedback on process, and helping the group to explore new tasks or issues. The main task of the leader will be to allow the team to be more creative and this may involve the phrasing of thought-provoking questions and giving the occasional steer but, above all, knowing when *not* to dominate and, having given a small steer, having the self-control to step back and let the team members take over. The motiva-tional effect of this form of behaviour lies in the fact that members will think that they have achieved everything themselves and will therefore be spurred on to attempt even greater feats.

4   Supportive coach

This approach involves a low level of knowledge input but a comparatively high level of intervention in the process of the team. Teams benefiting will be characterized by a general lack of confidence; they may be finding the task difficult or may not have a clear idea as to what to do next. Individuals within the team may be operating at different levels of confidence or ability.

Team leaders in these situations will need to do a great deal of looking and listening, they will need to know when to give encouragement, when to be helpful, and when to single out those in particular difficulty. They must be able to inspire trust and be willing to listen and empathize with people's feelings. They must also have the ability to question people's ability and understanding in a non-challenging way. While other approaches will motivate the team by challenge or stimulation, this approach will achieve motivation through a process of building and growing of confidence.

The four approaches to team motivation require flexibility of approach from the leader as well as an ability to judge a team at an individual level. It is probable, however, that there will be a tendency for teams to move towards requiring the creative group catalyst approach as they mature. The more a group are facilitated, the more it will become accustomed to drawing its own conclusions, and making its own decisions. It may be a harder group to manage but it will produce better results. In short, it will be a credit to its leader who, despite still facilitating and motivating, may by now be almost invisible.

WIFBs

At this stage it is worth while introducing another concept. The importance of looking for the WIFM has already been stressed and the approach to dealing with a low morale situation has consequently been person centred rather than business centred, but there are of course the demands of the business. These can be called the WIFBs (what is in it for the business) and should not be forgotten. After all, it is the business that is keeping the team in work, and often the harsh dictates of economic reality must prevail over the immediate feelings of the group. However, if you do insist that a course of action is necessary for the good of the business, do not forget your longer-term vision. Business needs must prevail, but if they are skilfully sewn into a compelling vision for the future, then people will accept current hardships as an investment for that future.

In dealing with either groups or individuals, the approach that the leader uses to influence or persuade others may arise as an issue. We must therefore look at the conscious, and often unconscious, ways that the leader sets out to persuade and influence. Once again we have the freedom to choose the style that best fits the situation and, again, the use or misuse of a style can be very motivating or demotivating.

Persuasion as part of motivation

In talking of persuasion we are really talking about power. Although in business the use of naked power is far more restricted than it once was, leaders still have power, although increasingly they are now wielding it by being skilfully persuasive.

A definition of persuasion that works well in the context of leadership is:

> 'The art of convincing others to do something that they would not otherwise do and to feel enthusiastic about doing so.'

In fact, if the persuasion is very skilful, the persuadee may then join forces with you in persuading others—this is the basis of the *apostolic principle*.

So how do leaders set out to persuade or influence others? Studies have shown that there are certain types of behaviour that are commonly used. Some leaders use these styles very powerfully while others use them to excess. The art is to appreciate which styles tend to come most naturally to you and then to consider whether that approach is likely to work on the person you are setting out to influence. There are clear links here to the philosophy of team motivation through the facilitation model outlined earlier.

The most common styles have been identified by a number of authors but, for simplicity, I will use the broad definitions made by Eales-White in *The Power of Persuasion*. An individual may set out to persuade someone else through the following: logic, incentives, empathy, or the group.

Logic

Those using this approach are usually skilled arguers, they have facts and arguments at their fingertips and will use them with power. They are assertive and will persist in their arguments. As they use facts and logic they are hard to beat in an argument: they will have prepared their ground well in advance and be hard to shake off their themes once started. Not surprisingly, a large number of senior people in business favour this approach; it has helped them to succeed and achieve their current positions.

The sort of expressions that the logical persuader will use are: 'The fact is. . .', 'Clearly the results of your doing that will be disastrous', 'What you say is illogical', ' Look at it my way and you will agree that the only rational action is. . . .'.

A main weakness of this approach is that users tend not to be good listeners and therefore may miss valuable information. They can also be bemused by the non-logical or emotional approach. The person who replies: 'I hear what you say but I just don't feel that way about it', is likely to throw them into confusion.

A classic example of a powerful logical persuader was Margaret Thatcher in her prime. Seldom, if ever, out-argued in Parliament, she eventually overused this approach and became notorious as a poor listener. People want to be talked to, not talked at!

Incentives

We have all experienced the boss who uses incentives to motivate and persuade us: 'Just keep on working like that and the bonus is as good as paid'. On the other hand you may have heard: 'If you are not for me you're against me'.

The leader who uses incentives takes a more emotional view of life than the logic user. This person believes that people will respond both to praise and to threats and so will use them. Those who agree with them tend to become one of the favoured in-crowd, while those who are not persuaded are made to feel that they have personally let the leader down and are now out of favour. These leaders may have favourites and also pet hates. They will believe in incentive bonus schemes because they fit into their belief patterns.

Some of the expressions they will use include: 'If you want that company car I would do it the way I suggest!' or 'That was a great job, come round to dinner next weekend!'

If this sounds somewhat negative, it is not meant to. We all use different approaches and these approaches are part of us. We do, however, need to know when to stop and when to change our approach. The use of incentives and praise can be an excellent motivator and very persuasive. It is when threat and criticism outweigh anything else that this approach is destructive.

STICK AND CARROT GONE MAD

When I was a young personnel officer I saw a classic case of the misuse of this style. In the mid seventies I worked for Rank Xerox and had responsibility for promulgating good HR policy in a number of sales offices. At this time the Employment Protection Act became legislation and this stated that everybody must have a minimum of one formal letter of warning before they could be dismissed for poor performance.

For some of our more Draconian sales managers this came as bad news and it was part of my job to tour sales offices to inform them of the legislation and to ask for their compliance with it. I visited one branch manager who had a reputation for being tough and was surprised when he listened intently without arguing and then told me how useful my visit had been.

I congratulated myself on having done a good job but was astounded to receive approximately 30 copy letters some days later. They all read along the following lines:

> Dear Joe/Mary/Peter . . .
>
> The purpose of this letter is to inform you that you are currently meeting all of your targets and that I am well pleased with your performance. Keep it up!
>   On the other hand, should you start to fall below this standard and fail to meet the targets, you will be liable for dismissal and you should take this letter as your first written warning.
>
> Yours

Not surprisingly, a near riot ensued. A clear example of an incentives approach in excess!

Empathy

Empathy is the ability to understand the thoughts and feelings of the other person. Being empathetic does not necessarily mean approving of the other person's viewpoint—you may consider it to be rubbish—but it does mean demonstrating to them that you understand 'where they are coming from'.

Empathy is being tuned in to the other person and being able to demonstrate that fact. For empathy to exist there must be trust and it must flow both ways. Therefore, to create trust, leaders must do a lot of listening, they must demonstrate an openness to the other's viewpoint and sometimes be prepared to discuss their own weaknesses or uncertainties in order to achieve a bonding. The empathetic approach to persuasion is slower than the others as it implies an investment of time from both sides. It may also lead to a more open exchange of views and therefore you may eventually arrive at a workable compromise that is agreeable to both sides.

If you have not got your own way completely, in other words there has been a compromise, the disadvantages of this must be balanced against the fact that your persuadee is probably genuinely committed to the revised proposal.

Some of the language that might be used with an empathetic approach might involve expressions such as: 'You must be very worried about that', 'Please tell me what you think about it', 'I know this project is important to you' or, 'I am no good at reading accounts, I would really appreciate your help here'.

So the empathetic approach involves trust and sometimes disclosures of weakness from the leader. It can be surprisingly powerful but, like the other approaches, can also be abused.

AN EMPATHETIC MANIPULATION

It is all too easy for the skilful manipulator to create false trust, to pretend to listen and even to reveal some weaknesses but then to abuse that trust once the other person has agreed to the proposal. I recall with wry amusement how the empathetic approach was used on a friend who worked for a major firm of accountants. Louise had responsibility for recruiting a large number of university graduates into the firm and part of this responsibility meant visiting academics and careers centres to inform them about the firm and the opportunities it offered. Her boss also had a responsibility for doing this but was far more interested in her work as a chartered accountant. Nevertheless a number of appointments were made for her to make these PR visits.

Louise often would receive a call from her boss shortly before she was due to make one of these visits and the conversation would run on the following lines: 'Hi, Louise. Look, I see from my diary that I've got to lunch one of these wretched professors tomorrow. Now, you know how bad I am at doing that. I find it so hard to talk to them and I soon run out of patience. You are so much better at talking to them than I am. I know you are busy but I think the firm would get much better value if you went.'

For the first few times she was extremely flattered by this approach and was sorry that her boss found it so hard to indulge in small talk. Later on she began to form a different opinion of what was going on, as time after time the approach was used to try to make her take on additional work.

Group

The leader who uses this approach has not only a strong attachment to the group but also a compelling vision of what can be achieved by it. In order to persuade either an individual or the group as a whole, the leader sets out to create exciting pictures of the future and what can be achieved if the persuadee agrees.

Leaders who use this approach are usually good with words, they like talking and they enjoy communicating their vision to others. In short, the message is: 'Join me. Look what we can achieve if you do so. We can create great things together. Just picture what it will be like.'

In business terms these words can refer to the turnaround of a business, the meeting of sales targets, the prosperity that will result if the unions will only agree to abandoning a restrictive practice, or the prestige that will follow if everybody works hard to achieve accreditation for total quality.

A MIXED BAG OF EXAMPLES

The appeal to the group vision is very powerful, especially when it meets the needs of those within the group. Because of this, it is often used by politicians when seeking to influence large numbers of people. A classic example of this approach can be seen in Martin Luther King who used emotive words to describe his particular vision: 'I have a dream!'

Of course this technique is not used just for the 'good'. Hitler was adept at it in talking of *Lebensraum* and painting a picture of a new Germany based on a Wagnerian myth. After Dunkirk, Churchill defied Hitler but used the same technique in his language. Britons had to pull together. 'I have nothing to offer but blood, toil, tears and sweat. . .' for everyone '. . . but we shall *never* surrender.'

If you have a leaning towards this technique you are probably already using it. You may be using it very effectively, but remember, if your vision or the images you create do not hit home and ring true, you may undermine your cause. A general manager within the Plessey Group was enthusiastically describing his vision for the future to a jaded staff consultative committee who felt that they had heard it all before. Eventually, the general manager stopped. 'Have I infected you with my enthusiasm for what we can achieve?' he asked. 'As far as we're concerned,' came the reply, 'that was a load of Domestos!'

A strategy for persuasion

In Chapter 6 we will look at the skills involved in handling the badly demotivated, or problem person. Before doing this it is important to put the four approaches into context by looking at a general strategy for persuasion which will involve the choice of the most appropriate style.

To be really persuasive you must be prepared, so a vital part of the strategy is your preparation:

1. *Work out your objectives*   You must be clear as to what you want to achieve.

2. *Think empathetically*   What does the other person want? What might be worrying him or her? Is there anything that you can offer that will help your argument to be accepted.

3. *Prepare your presentation*   This is not just the argument but also how you will deliver it. What will work in this case? Logic? Empathy? Appeal to group? Try to recall the sort of language that the other person uses. If he or she tends to use a particular approach, then it is likely that that approach will work on them.

The next stage is the meeting itself:

1. *Sound out the other person*   Ask questions and find out their views, this will help you to adjust your approach.

2. *Let them know your views*   Tell them *why* you hold them and discuss any objections they may have with them.

3. *Sell the benefits*   There will be good reasons for adopting your plan. Think in terms of the benefits that there may be for the other person rather than the plain features of your case. For example, if I am trying to sell you a house I may say that one of its features is that there are four bedrooms and two bathrooms. The benefit to you is that your in-laws can now come to stay with you for long periods.

4. *Make the other person curious*   If you can do this they will start to become involved despite themselves and involvement is a step towards commitment.

5. *Leave the other person a way out from his or her viewpoint*   If the other person's arguments are so comprehensively defeated that they feel mentally raped, they may continue to stick to their position as the only way of preserving their self-esteem. So, let them have their say and concede where they have a valid point. It does not mean that you will not get your own way in the end.

6. *Get agreement and then move on*   Once you have got the other person's agreement, agree to what you have decided and confirm any actions that the other person may now be committed to. Then break off the conversation. If you prolong it, the other person may change his or her mind and then you are back to square one again.

Summary

There are similarities between this strategy and selling. That is no surprise and the expression 'I need to sell her the idea' is often heard. Often, selling is confused with manipulation. This strategy is not manipulative so long as you believe in your proposal and put your case truthfully and ethically. This approach is about being effectively influential. Leaders cannot afford to be uninfluential as influence is a prerequisite to success.

Leadership is, by its very nature, about motivation and about influence. Leaders are persuaders and exert influence both as solo players as well as through teams. Growing an understanding of the motivation process is part of the leader's maturation; the mature leader motivates others and must understand the practical application of theory to do so effectively.

In addition, the leader must be able to pursue strategies of persuasion and must be able to communicate and be interpersonally effective to achieve success.

Your WIFMs from this chapter

- Are you *X* or *Y*? Would a change of attitude help relationships?

- Where are your people on the hierarchy of needs? Are you happy about their position?

- What can *you* do about your people's 'motivators'?

- What can you do to make your people's targets stretching yet motivating?

- Have you tested your people's morale? What can you do about it if it is low?

- Do you have someone you wish to persuade? Have you considered what persuasion approach they would find most attractive? Can you devise a strategy to use it?

Maturation

The interpersonal skills of the sensitive leader

We communicate the whole time; to cease communicating is to die. Consequently, the act of communicating comes so naturally to most of us that we ignore the fact that for our communication to be truly effective, it requires work, planning, and concentration. It is all too easy to fall into sloppy habits thus sowing the seeds of confusion in all directions.

In the preceding chapters we traced a path of birth and growth of leadership within the individual through a process of self-knowledge, followed by the development of both the vision and the team. The result of these processes was the motivation of other people. This section, however, is about the maturation of leadership and a major step in this maturation is the realization that effective communication is a vital aspect of the leader's role—an aspect that cannot be ignored.

This chapter, therefore, is about skills of communication; these include interpersonal skills that the leader must be aware of and must develop. While an emerging leader can be forgiven for concentrating on the development of the vision or on the formation and motivation of the team, leaders who wish to consolidate their position, and to mature within the role, cannot afford to neglect interpersonal skills. To some, these skills come naturally, but for many they are skills that require conscious development and practice.

The reason why practice is required relates to the fact that the process of communication itself is a minefield. The opportunities to 'get it wrong' are legion. George Bernard Shaw stated that: 'The greatest problem with communication is the illusion that it has been accomplished.' Perhaps that ironic statement sums up most of the pitfalls.

The need for skilful communication

Why is it so important for a leader to be an effective communicator? In Chapter 2, we examined the power base on which any leader must rely. One pillar of the power base was seen to be the leader's personal authority; this pillar relies very heavily on the way that the leader is able to handle other people. We also looked at WIST (wisdom, integrity, sensitivity, and tenacity) as an essential key to good leadership; the act of developing interpersonal and communication skills is a major step on the way to developing the W and S keys to effective leadership.

Effective communication is the crucial medium through which leaders achieve their aims. A short list of some of the key objectives that a leader might hold will show, without the need for further words, the need for effective communication to achieve them:

- Transmit the vision

- Motivate or persuade others

- Build the team

- Control the situation

- Develop others within their roles

- Help others cope with change and uncertainty

In fact, the development of particular skills to help others deal with the stresses of change may be one of the most vital skills required of leaders in the future.

Where the skills are needed

Effective leaders will have developed skills that add to their overall effectiveness with people. These skills will include talents in the following areas:

1. Questioning and listening.

2. The ability to read the less obvious messages sent. Messages of body language and the meaning behind the words being spoken.

3. The sensitivity to identify the causes of conflict and to map routes towards its resolution by an understanding of what may be stimulating the other person's supposedly bizarre behaviour.

These skills are about obtaining information and processing it correctly. They also enable the leader to end up with the right data, as information, whether received or transmitted, is power. However, the process of communication between two people often starts with the best of intentions but ends in failure. Why?

The process of communication is about transmitting and receiving so we need to look at both of these areas before communication, in its entirety, can be understood.

Transmitting and receiving—the opportunities and pitfalls

When we set out to communicate or influence we adopt behaviours to enable that communication to take place. Often we get it right and the message is received, understood, and acted upon. Equally often, it appears that something goes wrong with the process, the message is misunderstood and sometimes generates the exact opposite response to that which is desired. What has gone wrong?

On an individual level, the scope for misunderstanding can be explained by referring to a strange paradox of communication. This is the paradox of *intention–behaviour–impact* (a theme that also underlies the LIFO® model explained in Chapter 8). What does it mean?

Before I start to communicate I have an intention. This intention may be to show interest, show sympathy, give an instruction, or give an explanation. The reasons may be legion! However, the intention must be expressed in behaviour and spoken words or it will simply remain as thoughts in my mind.

The moment I start to express my intention to someone else is when the problems may begin, as the words I use to express myself, or the way in which I say them, may give an entirely different impression to that intended. Consequently, the impact of my communicated intention may be light years away from that which was intended.

That is the paradox, it explains why so many people misread each other and why it is so necessary to plan and analyse your communication, its purpose, and method, before embarking on it. We may not always be seen or interpreted as we would wish to be seen or interpreted.

The Scottish Bard, Robert Burns, came close to the truth when he stated: 'O wad some Pow'r the giftie, To see oursels as others see us.'

THE BOTCHED COACHING SESSION

The departmental manager wishes to train his subordinate in a new method of filling in a form dealing with summaries of financial transactions. The subordinate has several years' experience as an accounts clerk. It is the intention of the manager to pass on the information in as pleasant and efficient a manner as possible.

Manager: 'Good morning, Phyllis. Now I want to show you how we are going to enter the accounts summaries, in future. Well, the first thing we do is open form X at page two. That's right, well done. Now the next thing we do is look at these two columns marked 'Debits' and 'Credits'. You will remember that debits represent money going out (and we don't like that, do we?) while credits represent money coming in. Got that, dear? So, now in our neatest handwriting we are going to make an entry in the debit column. Phyllis, why are you looking so fed up? Phyllis?'

The intention was good but the behaviour was patronizing and totally unfitting towards a fellow adult who probably knew more about the procedure than he did. The impact was to demotivate the hapless accounts clerk rather than motivate her.

The paradox illustrates how communication can fail at one level. It is now necessary to look at the process and the skills involved in order to see how a better understanding can help the maturing leader avoid the many traps along the way.

The process—opportunities for getting it right

A more detailed and sophisticated extrapolation of the intention–behaviour–impact conundrum is the following model of transmission and receipt of information: *idea–code–transmit–receive–decode–interpret*

1. *The idea*   Before communication starts the communicator must have a motive or an idea. The motive may be simple or complex but it remains only a thought until it is expressed.

2. *Code*   When the idea is expressed it must be put into words. The words may be spoken or written but they carry the essential information contained in the message. Often it is difficult for people to express emotions or complex motives, and thus it is in the process of putting ideas into words that the leader can first start to go wrong.

3. *Transmission*   This is the medium for the message. Is it to be spoken or is it to be put into writing? The leader in a business situation needs to select the medium carefully. How is the receiver likely to react to different media? What will catch the other person's attention or, even more important, actively stimulate the other person's interest? When the message is launched towards the recipient, it is being transmitted.

4. *Reception*   The intended receivers of the message may or may not know what to expect, but will certainly have a number of feelings, attitudes, or prejudices of their own. If, for example, they

are expecting instructions, they may have concerns about their ability to fulfil them. Therefore, whatever is going on in the receivers' minds may either help or hinder the reception of the message.

In addition, a number of external distractions, such as interruptions, noisy offices, or competing messages, can add to the likelihood of the message not being received as clearly as you would wish.

5. *Decode*   Once the message has been received it must be translated by the receiver into words and concepts that have meaning for them. It is in this process of decoding that some of the main dangers lie. Do words mean the same thing to different people? Do my expectations predispose me to interpret the message in a particular way? The possibilities for misunderstanding are endless.

6. *Interpretation*   This is the final stage and is largely dependent on what has gone on in the preceding five stages. Although the responsibility for good communication largely rests with the sender, it is a sad truism that some people 'Just hear what they want to hear, and disregard the rest' (Paul Simon).

If we think too hard about the above process we may wonder how any communication ever takes place successfully. The following two (true) extracts from newspapers show how easy it is for innocent words to create a totally wrong picture.

Letter in *The Yorkshire Observer*

Sir, It gives me great pleasure to be able to tender you my good wishes for the future progress of your most popular morning paper, *The Yorkshire Observer*, without which I should not be satisfied, for it is half my breakfast.

Extract from *Los Angeles South-West News*

Word was received last week that Mrs Gertrude Higgins, teacher of the 36th Street School, was severely bitten by a dog on the school grounds. Principal Gail Mahoney observed that it could just as easily have been a child.

Avoiding the communication traps—conversation management

As mentioned earlier, there are a variety of skills that the maturing leader can deploy in order to become a better communicator, augment his or her power base, and be seen to be interpersonally sensitive. These are key skills as, if leadership is about the reactions between the leader and followers, then good communication is a bastion of the leader's legitimate authority. It is necessary to examine these skills in order to show how they can be applied effectively. However, as real skill can only be developed by practice rather than by reading, so the challenge to increase interpersonal effectiveness must remain with the reader.

The core skill that brings together and blends all the techniques that are described below could be called *conversation management* as it is the skill of extracting every ounce of value from the conversation or communication that is taking place by using a number of talents that involve the use of eyes, ears, brain, and intuition. Most managers can control the length and breadth of a conversation but it is only truly perceptive leaders who can use skills that enable them to see *within* the conversation, to sort out meanings, to perceive the unobvious, and to establish what is really being said.

Conversation management—questioning skills

Many leaders do not obtain good information as they do not know how to ask for it correctly. Those with whom you communicate may be so caught up in their own agendas that they unwittingly fail to give you the most relevant information. On the other hand, they may simply not know what you want and therefore cannot help you unless your questions, and the way in which they are asked, allow them to do so.

A variety of effective questioning techniques exist and an examination of the most valuable ways will offer the basis of effective conversation management.

Closed or open questions

It is in the understanding of the difference between these two sorts of questions that good questioning starts.

A closed question is asked in such a way that it elicits only a 'Yes' or 'No' answer. Examples of such questions might be: 'Is it raining today?' or 'Have you finished the monthly sales report?' Questions such as this are fine when you simply want to establish or confirm facts. They are less useful when you need to probe deeper.

Open questions, on the other hand, allow the questioner to open up whole subject areas, to test assumptions, to establish the emotions involved, and to make vital connections. The questioner can get into an open question mode by starting questions with words like: why, when, how, or what. These questioning words force the reply to be both longer and specific. For example, the closed questions outlined above could be turned into: 'How do you feel about the weather today?' (there could be various replies to this), or 'What are your main conclusions from the monthly sales report?'

There is one phrase, however, that takes the questioner more powerfully into open questions than any other. That is the phrase, *'tell me'*. Without further ceremony these simple words force the other person into opening up and giving information, facts, or opinion. 'Tell me about the sales figures.' 'Tell me about the atmosphere in the factory at present.'

On a training programme in recruitment skills a trainer was having a hard time persuading a number of cynical managers of the benefits of asking questions in a planned, considered way. It was the second day of the programme and one course member in particular appeared distracted and disinterested. The trainer realized that this was in part due to the fact that the participant's car had been broken into the previous evening and the radio, with a number of cassettes, had been stolen. Eventually the participant stated sullenly, 'I can't see the difference between open and closed questions and what's the point, anyway?'

Suddenly the trainer had a flash of inspiration. 'Was your car burgled last night?' he asked.

'Yes', came the guarded reply.

'Now,' said the trainer, 'tell me how you feel about the fact that your car was burgled.'

The participant stood up and made a violent gesture with both hands.

'I want to strangle the rat that did it!' he shouted. He then smiled sheepishly.

'I think I get the point', he demurred.

Funnelling, or moving from broad brush to specific

One of the most useful skills in conversation management is that of being able to ask increasingly specific open and closed questions in order to obtain the very best information. It is a technique that is often used in recruitment interviews but it can be applied to most conversations with a purpose.

The technique of *funnelling* is to ask as broad based a question as possible in connection with the subject under discussion and then, by asking increasingly specific questions, to narrow the scope of the conversation so that you are finally posing very specific and demanding questions in the area that you have been able to identify as being of most interest.

The benefits of this approach are that:

1. The other person initially sets the starting point which enables you to see what their priorities may be.

2. As questions are answered you can make hypotheses about the other person's character or motives. Your intuition is given free rein and is subsequently subjected to test as the conversation progresses.

3. When your questions become more specific, you can apply subtle pressure. The more often then that your intuition tells you something about the other person, the more likely it is to be right and to stand up to your own testing.

The following extract from a recruitment interview shows the funnelling process in operation. The interviewee is a university undergraduate being interviewed for his first job. Often hypotheses and intuition play a greater part in graduate recruitment than in other spheres, simply because the average graduate has no record of employment from which to make judgements.

THE RECRUITMENT INTERVIEW

INTERVIEWER: We've talked about your degree course, but now tell me about your vacations, Toni.

TONI: Well, I've done the usual thing of interrailing around Europe but last vacation I took a job.

INTERVIEWER: That's interesting, what sort of job did you take?

TONI: I worked in an electrical components factory for three months.

INTERVIEWER: Now there are several businesses in your district where you might have worked, why did you decide to go there?

TONI: My father is a solicitor and my mother an accountant, both offered me work experience in their offices but I felt that it would be more useful for me to see how the 'other half' lives and works by taking the job in the factory.

INTERVIEWER: (*Making the hypothesis that this person is independent and likes a challenge*) OK, but tell me, how did they take to you in the factory? They must have thought you were very different.

TONI: At first, they did not know what to make of me and were rather suspicious so I went out of my way to convince them that I was an ordinary person and not some stuck-up student.

INTERVIEWER: (*Testing the hypothesis*) How did you do that?

TONI: I made sure that I always had lunch with my workmates and also went out to the pub with them on Fridays. They soon accepted me.

INTERVIEWER: (*Becoming more specific*) What was your actual work in the factory?

TONI: My job was to obtain materials from the stores and make sure that the assembly lines were always supplied.

INTERVIEWER: (*Wishing to test a hypothesis that Toni is a determined person with a closed question*) Did things always run smoothly for you in doing this?

TONI: Not always .

INTERVIEWER: What happened?

TONI: Sometimes I was given the wrong materials and the operators who were on piece work became quite angry.

INTERVIEWER: (*Becoming very specific in order to retest*) Give me a situation where this happened and tell me what you did to sort it out.

Thus, in taking the other person down a path, the interviewer has been able to make use of the information as it arrives to make hypotheses and launch increasingly specific questions both to gather further information and to test out the hypotheses. The S in WIST can thus be tested to add to the leader's W.

The reflective question

This is as much a statement as a question but it has the same effect of allowing you to make and test hypotheses. It is, in fact, one of the most powerful tools in the leader's kitbag as it allows you to test your intuition on the other person as well as to demonstrate empathy in many cases.

The technique is to listen hard to what may be the main emotion or motive hinted at in what the other person is saying, and then to reflect that back at them in a short question or statement of how you perceive what they have been saying. If you get that restatement right this can have a powerful effect on the other person as they suddenly become aware that their listener understands them and is on the same wavelength.

Once again, examples can illustrate the point better than abstraction:

1. *Statement*   Well our supplier says that the components will be delivered on time and I suppose she knows what she is talking about.
   Reflective question   (Picking up on the doubt and uncertainty in the statement) But you have some doubts.

2. *Statement*   I have to tell you, my supervisor is always picking on me for the most trivial reasons.
   Reflection   You consider yourself to be hard done by?

Equally powerful as a reflection is the one word question. By picking on one emotive word in the speaker's sentence it is possible to demonstrate great understanding and thereby unlock a great deal more information. For example:

1. *Statement*   I had been so happy in the engineering department until the take-over and all these new procedures were brought in. I find the newest proposals absolutely *terrifying*.
   Reflection   Terrifying?

Or, a different way of answering example 2, above. This time not demonstrating empathy, but in its place, authority and scepticism:

Reflection   Trivial?

Conversation management—the flow of information

Good conversation management should produce a steady stream of useful information that flows towards the leader. To ask effective questions is like turning on a tap—information, like water, starts to flow. Good questions, however, are of little use unless the answers are listened to with the same level of skill. If questions turn on the tap of information, it is good listening that will keep the flow coming and may even increase it.

The art of powerful listening

The first thing to note about listening is that it is not a passive activity but an active one. Furthermore, the power base within the conversation often rests with the listener rather than the speaker. The listener has power simply by being in the position of listener and can turn the imaginary tap off or on solely by exercising good or poor listening skills.

It is also important to realize that there is more to being a good listener than just being attentive. The skills involved include the following demanding activities:

- Exercise of concentration

- Searching for key words and patterns

- Interpretation and positive use of body language

It you are a leader who is able to use all these skills to sort, process and, above all, *understand* the information flowing towards you then not only will you feel more confident but you will also be felt by others to be both effective and approachable.

THE INSENSITIVE LEADER

A young man who worked as a project manager in a division of GEC used to become extremely agitated at what he felt were the poor listening skills of his boss, a divisional manager. The boss used to request all reports and recommendations in writing so that they could be discussed after he had had an opportunity to read them.

The divisional manager would then telephone the project manager when he felt ready to discuss the reports and ask him to come and see him. However, in the five minutes that it took the young manager to reach his office, the divisional manager would often have become interested in something else and would be deeply into some other document.

The conversation would start with the project manager explaining his recommendations while the divisional manager gradually withdrew his attention by first glancing at the other document and then slowly becoming increasingly absorbed in it until he appeared to be concentrating on it to the exclusion of what the project manager had to tell him.

This used to so unnerve the young project manager that he used to 'dry up' in mid-sentence. At this stage the senior manager would say brusquely, 'Go on, I am listening!' Eventually, after several such non-conversations, the young junior manager plucked up the courage to tackle his boss on his listening skills.

'You know,' he said, 'I find it almost impossible to talk when you are so obviously concentrating on something else.' The divisional manager then stated that he was one of those lucky people who are able to concentrate on two things at once and gave him a reasonably accurate summary of the situation under discussion. Although nonplussed by this, the project manager insisted that this method of listening was a major barrier to him and that he would be able to talk more rationally and forcefully if he felt he had the other person's undivided attention. Reluctantly his boss relented.

Making use of the skills

1. Exercise of concentration

When in conversation with someone, the greatest compliment that you can pay them is to listen carefully and attentively. But what does this mean? For a start, this means that, if the conversation is private and serious in nature, it is courteous to make sure that it is undisturbed and that instruments of interruption, such as the telephone, are banned. This may mean moving out of your office to somewhere private, and the physical act of doing so may relax the other person or at least convince him or her that the conversation is being taken seriously.

Next, give the other person your undivided attention. Many listeners go through long conversations with their own agendas firmly in the forefront of their minds and then wonder why they do not have all the information they expected to have at the end of it.

Do not enter a conversation with the purpose of thinking up questions as it develops. Thinking of questions will distract you from listening and getting the facts. People often try to invent questions with the purpose of showing how intelligent or informed they are rather than that of clarifying the issue. So, try not to think up questions. The unforced questions that occur to you are likely to be far more powerful and perceptive; they are also more likely to clarify the issue for you.

Giving the other person your undivided attention means exercising concentration, banning daydreams and not trying to 'top' the story with a better one of your own. If your time is limited, tell the other person how long you have but then pay the compliment of giving your undivided attention to the speaker for that space of time. One CEO of a major public company had a wonderful reputation as a listener. He would say, 'I can only give you ten minutes but they will be *your ten minutes* and we may be able to solve your problem in that time.'

2. Searching for key words and patterns

The words that people use, the way in which they are spoken, and the different patterns in which they are used often give clues as to what may be on their minds. The use of words may also hint at real meaning or emotion behind what is being said. The effective listener looks for the patterns, tries to make the connections, and sets out to find the real message.

Much of the valuable work on listening comes from those involved in occupational counselling and Tony Milne, founder of CEPEC, The Centre for Professional Employment Counselling, states that many people will *distort, delete* or *generalize* when in conversation. They are more likely to do this when stressed or when talking to someone in authority—the leader. The effective leader needs to use sophisticated listening skills to overcome this editing and these skills may be found in searching for one of the following three elements:

The core of the sentence

The easiest way to listen attentively is to seek the word that the speaker emphasizes most within the sentence. Sometimes this emphasis may be only slight, but if the speaker is agitated it may be very pronounced. The word that receives the emphasis becomes the *core* or pivotal part of the sentence. It has the job of carrying the speaker's intention and meaning. For example, take this sentence 'I did not mishandle that negotiation ' and consider the two different meanings that can be given to it simply by giving emphasis to either the third or the fifth word.

People use emphasis either to stress meaning or to disguise it. An emotive statement like 'I never said he was a lousy manager' is open to multiple interpretations and must be listened to carefully in order to sort out what is really on the speaker's mind. In fact in the case of this sentence as many different meanings can be deduced as there are words in the sentence.

Pointer words

In any language there are a number of words or expressions that are used either to reinforce a point, or as infillers. When used in the correct way they have their own particular meaning, but when the word appears to have no real part in the construction of the sentence you should ask yourself why it is there and whether it is being used to disguise or conceal something else. Words like 'actually', 'naturally', and 'obviously' are innocuous in themselves, but can be used subtly and to great effect.

Consider the following two sentences:

> The only place to buy a suit is Savile Row.

and:

> 'I will be found at Wimbledon in June.'

If 'naturally' or 'obviously' were to be added to either sentence a whole new dimension of implied snobbery or social 'put down' creeps in. After all 'where else does one obtain good suits and if that is not obvious to you, then you can't be one of us!'

On the other hand, the word 'actually' can be used to disguise embarrassment. It often has no valid part to play in the construction of a sentence but still occurs. How often have you heard someone say something like: 'I'm afraid I've not finished the report, actually' or 'Actually, I'm now over budget.' So, if a word does not appear to have a functional part in the construction of a sentence, ask yourself why it is there and hypothesize as to what it may be concealing.

Finally, one expression that is often used as a screen is the phrase 'sort of'. This is a favourite expression in the English language and I am sure that other languages and cultures have their own versions. When used in a sentence such as 'As the day dawned a sort of haze indicated fine weather to come.' the expression is innocuous. However, when used in a sentence such as 'The project is sort of overrunning' it may be being used as a decoy. The real message may be 'The project is seriously behind schedule.' The fact is that things do not 'sort of' overrun. They either overrun or they do not!

If you find 'sort of' being used in the wrong context, challenge it—this will probably lead you to the real facts. I once had the job of quizzing a manager on the reasons why his performance was deteriorating. During the conversation he was elusive, but new information came to light; it transpired that he was now living in London, a longer journey to work. When I asked him why he was now in London he replied, 'Well, since my wife and I sort of split up, it seemed the best thing to do.' 'Sort of?' I challenged. To my distress, the manager then broke down in tears. It transpired that he was totally unable to come to terms with the situation and that it was this, rather than anything else, that was affecting his work.

Patterns

Look for words that reoccur or that are on the same theme. Why should this be? Do these words point to some underlying fear or expectations? The concept of the Freudian slip is well known but could a reoccurring pattern be more than that? Could it be a signal of something that the speaker may consciously or unconsciously be attempting to conceal? The following bizarre example is told by Tony Milne of CEPEC.

THE PRERETIREMENT ENIGMA

An organization used to send all its employees to a preretirement counsellor at the start of their final year's work before retirement. The counsellor's work was to ask them questions and to ensure that they were mentally prepared for this major change in their lives.

One man who was seen by the counsellor appeared to be well prepared. He said that he had worked for the organization for many years and was now looking forward to retirement. He saw it as an opportunity to see more of his grandchildren, catch up with some travelling, and finally, to get to grips with the garden.

The counsellor reported back that there were no problems and forgot about the man. To his surprise the company contacted him some months later asking him to reinterview the man, as they now felt something was wrong but could not work out what it was.

During the conversation the counsellor asked an open question: 'Tell me how you now feel about your retirement.' The answer he received included a number of expressions such as: 'I just can't see the way ahead', 'The future is a blank to me', 'I'm in a fog as to what to do.'

No other information was forthcoming until the counsellor realized that all these expressions had the common theme of lack of sight. From this the counsellor hypothesized that there was something wrong with the man's sight and, challenged with this hypothesis, he confessed. It transpired that the man was going blind and the irony was that the impending blindness, which had not been diagnosed previously, would strike shortly after the retirement.

The man, being proud, had not wanted the sympathy of his colleagues and wished to retire normally and then move out of the area. He was unable to escape the cruel irony that dictated that he would be unable to enjoy his leisure fully when finally he had it. Although he tried to hide the situation, his feelings about it slipped out in the usage and patterns of his words.

Words are like beacons, they point the way to finding out what is going on in the other person's heart or mind. Beacons can however be false signals, placed with the deliberate intention of misdirection. Sensitive leaders listen carefully, suspend judgement, and then draw the best conclusions based on skilful use of their ears. Sensitive leaders also use their eyes.

Conversation management—interpretation and positive use of body language

Much has been spoken and written about the subject of body language and it would be foolhardy to attempt too definitive a description of the many signals that we all project all the time. Alan Pease in *Body Language* gives an amusing and thorough description of the signals covering a wide range of situations. In this section only a few areas that are of extreme importance for a leader to understand are analysed. If you have a particular interest in this field you should read further and consider studying the applications of neuro linguistic programming (NLP).

Use of body language to improve the flow of communication

A technique often used by professional listeners is that of *mirroring*. This involves looking at the overall body posture of the person speaking to you and then adopting a similar posture. For example, if the other person leans forward intently then do the same. If the other person lounges back in a relaxed manner, adopt a similar position. The message given by doing this, that the listener is empathetic, is a physical demonstration, as in the other person's subconscious a message is triggered that the listener is more like them or more in congruence with them, than not.

If you want to test this idea out then start a conversation and get the other person to talk to you at length and in detail. For part of the conversation deliberately mirror the speaker's overall body posture; you should find that the conversation flows smoothly. Then, deliberately de-mirror the speaker's posture; if you adopt a closed position with arms folded, head down and body turned slightly away from the speaker, you should find that the other person's conversation becomes stilted and then begins to dry up.

Signals of lying and decision-making

When trying to influence someone, or when someone is trying to influence you, it is vital to know when the other person is lying or when they are starting to make up their mind about your proposition. When dealing with body language it is also necessary to accept that the signals may be indications and not definitive proof of what is going on in the other person's mind. However, there is usually enough substance, given the circumstances of the conversation, to pursue and test your hypotheses.

Lies are usually accompanied by two forms of behaviour. The liar may stroke his or her upper lip with a forefinger as a lie is delivered. This gesture originates from childhood when young children often cover the entire mouth as they deliver a real 'whopper'. The other give-away is to brush either real or imaginary specks of fluff or dirt from clothing while speaking. This is a subliminal gesture, the liar is trying to generate distance from the words being spoken.

The process of decision-making is often indicated by the following sequence of actions. While the proposition is being considered the other person is likely to hold his or her head to one side with one hand supporting it. The index finger will be straight and rest on the cheek, pointed upwards. The other fingers will cradle the chin—this is often a signal that the other person is interested and evaluating, but has not yet reached a decision. As the individual starts to make a decision, the index finger will join the others and start to stroke the chin. This usually means that interested evaluation is giving way to decision-making.

Observe people on television, especially those being interviewed, and make your own conclusions about what they are saying. It is extremely difficult to suppress body language and only those who have had sophisticated media training do so successfully.

Signs of distress and aggression

A leader often has to confront issues and persuade others to do what they are unwilling to tackle. The reactions will often be one of distress and sometimes of downright hostility. It is vital to understand the true effect of your words or actions, especially as others will not always wish to disclose their real feelings to you. Once you have picked up the real message it is then possible to adjust your own behaviour so as to obtain the most from the situation.

Acute distress is often accompanied by the individual bringing his or her hand up to the side of the neck and caressing the neck with the palm of the hand. The other arm may then be placed across the chest in a protective blocking gesture. If you are speaking to someone and they start to show these signs you have probably touched a nerve. What you say next is up to you, but be aware of their discomfort.

Aggression is easier to spot and is more usually accompanied by angry words. Be less worried by those who go red in the face and bluster at you; the main thrust of their anger is over. However, those who go pale, who suck in their cheeks and then point an index finger at you while speaking are very angry, perhaps violently so. This is the time to back off, or duck!

Using communication skills to handle conflict

In looking at body language we have observed the outward signs of aggression. But what are its causes? Why does conflict occur?

In Chapter 8 we will look at how the stresses of change can make people act in seemingly bizarre ways and we will examine a framework for assessing what drives the other person. Here, however, we will concentrate on *why* conflict occurs and how it can be handled through the effective use of interpersonal skills.

Causes of conflict

Conflict situations in the workplace arise for a broad variety of reasons. Root causes may be the different vested interests of people, causing them to draw different conclusions from the same message. The message can be warped by other people who may hear what they want to hear. In the end, however, it is up to you as leader to unscramble the message and to move ahead towards the achievement of your objectives. The message can be warped by any of the following:

1. *Different perceptions*   Situations may seem threatening or trivial depending on from where in the organization they are viewed.

2. *Value judgements*   Everybody makes them all the time. Indeed we tend to be influenced by other people's value judgements when they speak to us about how they perceive things.

3. *Assumptions*   The quickest way to get it wrong is to assume it. The old joke says that, broken down, the word assume makes an '*ass* out of *u* and *me*'. How very true, but assumptions can also lead to conflict.

4. *Jealousy*   One of the most destructive of the seven deadly sins and it is alive, well, and living in most organizations. It is difficult to deal with jealousy as its sources may stem from deep down inside the individual involved and it can lead to very negative behaviour. But jealousy can be identified if you make informed hypotheses.

5. *Feeling under threat*   Lucky are those who survive their careers without ever feeling threatened. A basic instinct is to fight to survive. Organizational conflict follows.

6. *Being left out*   Those who do not consider themselves to have any part in the decision-making process make the wrong inferences, react too soon to events, and may initially be afraid to ask questions about what is going on.

Any one or more of these factors can result in an explosive mixture and the leader needs to have a communications strategy available to help untangle the causes of the conflict. Once unravelled, the root causes can be tackled.

A mental checklist for the strategy should follow these lines:

1. What form does the conflict take and what are my objectives in trying to defuse it? What do I want to achieve?

2. Is the conflict destructive? Not all conflict is bad and it may simply be a necessary part of a transition process.

3. What is the best time and place to speak to the other person(s)? Does this mean my territory, their territory, or neutral ground?

4. How can I best adjust to this person? If the personal chemistry is unhelpful, can I adjust my approach to increase empathy without compromising my position?

5. How will I best put my case into words? Where will I start, what is the most logical sequence? What should be included and excluded and, given my knowledge of the other party, what are the most suitable words to use?

6. Remember to listen. Poor listening will antagonize while good listening which is reinforced by many checks of understanding may defuse the situation.

7. Finally, how far can I expect to get in one conversation? Do not expect to get immediate agreement, it may follow after a short gap during which the other person seeks and finds ways of saving face.

The causes and strategy outlined above do not attempt to deal with situations where two individuals just seem to have nothing in common, where there is no mutual understanding, or where the interpersonal chemistry appears totally wrong. Leaders do have a responsibility, however, to be good leaders regardless of the chemistry, and so further analysis of what may be thought of as the other party's unreasonable behaviour will be examined later. The ambiguity and stress of change usually exacerbates antipathy and so the driving forces of both normal and excessive behaviour will be revisited in Chapter 8.

Summary

Leaders must communicate to achieve their aims. Effective communication, however, is something that does not come naturally to everybody—it is something that requires work and concentration. There are pitfalls in the communication process that can mean that the impact of the message is very different from its intended effect. Through conversation management, skilled questioning and listening, and interpretation of both body language and words, the leader can become more expert with people—a vital part of the maturation process.

Your WIFMs from this chapter

- How much of your time do you devote to communicating with other people?

- How seriously do you treat communication?

- How often do you consciously choose a particular method of asking questions?

- Do you really listen? What do you listen for?

- Do you try to analyse the non-verbal messages when you are speaking to someone?

- If you are in a conflict situation with someone, have you fully analysed the causes?

Giving away your power

Introduction

The concept of power is a preoccupation for many leaders. For some it is a drug and for others it is a source of fascination. In earlier chapters I examined the sources of a leader's power and so it may seem strange that the central focus of this chapter is *'giving it away'*. However, the concept of giving away one's power is both a demand made on us if we are leaders in the work situation and a choice that is open to us. *We* invent most of the constraints.

It is a strange paradox that in order to keep hold of something, it is necessary to give of it. This certainly applies to the important things in life such as love and happiness. Debatably, it also applies to other factors such as wealth. The selfish lover, who clings to a loved one and sees the relationship as one of possession rather than of mutual sharing, will almost certainly lose that loved one, just as the rich miser descends into a multifaceted poverty by hoarding wealth and becoming its victim rather than its beneficiary. On the other hand, those who desperately seek happiness are often counselled to work with those who are worse off than they are, and in the act of giving happiness to others, often find it for themselves.

So it is with leadership. The leader who clings to power, who is afraid to give it to others, will in fact cease to be a leader. In business, this person will increasingly become ineffective and in the end will be ousted, while in politics it is the leader's relationship to power that makes the difference between a legitimate leader and a tyrant. Tyrants do, of course, retain their power for a time, but people who are hated and feared by their followers, who go to elaborate lengths to protect themselves from them, such as Saddam Hussein and Nicolae Ceaușescu, may be in control but are *not* leaders. In fact, those who have learnt to rely on their hierarchical position as a basis for power are those most likely to find it difficult to adjust to the concept of power deriving from the ability to develop others.

The concept of power addiction will be examined more closely in Chapter 9, where the subject of failure in leaders will be the central theme. For the present, suffice it to say that in history it is those leaders who have deliberately chosen to give away their power and to serve their followers who have left the most powerful images and who, in fact, have had the longest lasting effect. Stalin wielded power like the proverbial hammer on an anvil, yet his work was rapidly being dismantled after only a few short years. He has left no such powerful image as a legacy to history as either Ghandi confronting the British government with little other than a loincloth, wisdom, and pacifism, or Christ kneeling to wash the feet of his Apostles. 'He also serves who leads.'

So how do you give away your power?

THE NON-SERVING, EGO LEADER

In large legal practices it is often common for an articled clerk to share an office with a partner in the firm; this is known as 'Having a seat with'. The intention is that the partner should give the trainee work but also coach, train, and develop the trainee. From my experience of training solicitors, I had become quite familiar with this custom and was under the impression that it usually worked quite well, although some solicitors were more sought after by trainees than others.

I did, however, meet a Partner in one firm, who boasted that trainees avoided having a seat with him whenever possible. He stated that it was his intention to make them work while they were with him. Explanations about 'how' or 'why' took second place to getting the work out. If this meant that the trainee spent large parts of the week idle because the solicitor did not do a briefing, then so be it. The solicitor actually took pride in the fact that he bullied his trainees and was a hard taskmaster when he did get round to assigning tasks. 'It's amazing how lacking in initiative the average trainee is,' he declared. 'Still they know not to come to me with any damn fool questions.'

One of his partners informed me that he was avoided because in that practice he was regarded not only as a dinosaur, but also as a pompous ass.

Assessing your power—What and how to give

In Chapter 2, major sources of a leader's power—positional, personal, and expert—were examined. The first step then is to examine where you think the basis of your power as leader lies and to consider ways in which that power can be shared with subordinates in order to enrich their work and make them more effective.

This does certainly not mean that you should consider giving someone else your job (there is no point in being naive). However, it is a case of examining areas where you are powerful and considering whether and how you could pass on aspects of that power to someone else to make that person more effective, more useful, and more *empowered* for the common good.

Traditional thinking about power assumes that if some increase their power then others must automatically lose power. This does not have to be the case; just as effectively working teams can achieve synergy, so can the effective sharing of power enable the whole team, department, or organization to be more powerful, more productive, and more creative. In this chapter, the following methods of empowering and enabling others will be examined:

- Challenging others to achieve excellence

- Delegation of tasks and authority

- Coaching skills

- Facilitation

There should be two key results from the above:

- A move towards what is known as the 'learning organization'.

- Sophisticated followership

These results will be examined and explained, as well as the probable personal results for you.

Challenging others to achieve excellence

It is a prime duty of leaders, at any level of an organization, to insist on excellence from others. In fact, it could be argued that someone who tolerates mediocrity is not a leader but is in collusion with others for the attainment of second best.

A CRYPTIC FAREWELL

A young manager, when moving to another organization, was bemused to find written on her leaving card, among the many bland wishes of good luck, the following cryptic message from her boss:'Be hard to please!' When the time came for final goodbyes she asked her former boss why he had written that particular message.

'I could have written the usual message wishing you good luck and saying we will miss you,' came the reply, 'but that is so obvious that it does not need stating. I wanted to leave you with something really worth while, and you will remember that there have been occasions when I have almost driven you crazy by insisting that certain jobs were done just that little bit better. You did not always thank me at the time but my insistence has caused us both to achieve more than either of us would initially have thought possible. So, take my advice—be hard to please!'

The young manager adopted that advice as a personal mission statement: it took her a long way.

It is perhaps one of the tragedies of life that so many people who, in their private lives, take important decisions, organize complex events, or hold positions that demand responsibility and the need to work through others do not exhibit these talents in their place of work. Are they expected to have left their brains and initiative at home? During my years in industry and commerce I have been amazed at the number of so-called ordinary people who have achieved great things outside work but who have not thought to show initiative, design new systems, or question decisions while at work.

I have known a high-ranking Conservative councillor whose job simply involved clerical work, and an inspiring youth group leader who performed menial work on a sales ledger. In the same export sales office in a part of the Fisons Group, two sales clerks sat opposite each other: one was one of the world's leading authorities on ferns, with several species named after him while the other was a respected poet. The organization treated them in a strictly 'tell' style and never once asked them what they thought. What a waste!

It must be one of the prime functions of leaders at all levels to discover and liberate the talents of those who work for them. A phrase coined by Warren Bennis is that 'good leaders let other leaders lead'. Another way of putting it is that leaders *must* look for the talent in others, and allow it to grow. The essence is that good leaders must grow other leaders and put themselves out to do so.

It is, of course, easy to say this but harder to do it. The actual methods will be examined later in this chapter but for now, the following words may help:

Challenge   Support   Acknowledge

- Challenge others to do better

- Support them when they try

- Thank, praise and give feedback

Figure 7.1 illustrates how this syndrome can work. Many workers reach what they regard as their highest level of competence. They know how to do the work. It is difficult for people to continue to achieve excellence indefinitely thereafter and a decline in output, quality, or commitment

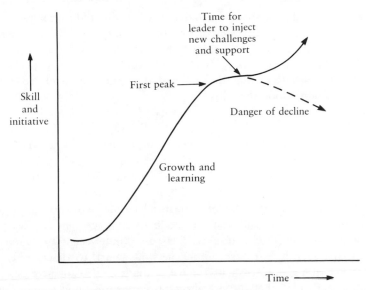

Figure 7.1   The challenge–support–acknowledge syndrome

often follows. Can the leader anticipate the decline and at the vital moment give new tasks, ask them to take on projects at a higher level and give them support and encouragement when they do so? If this is possible, then the overall effectiveness of that person (to say nothing of their enjoyment) should be launched onto a higher plane.

An example of this sort of leadership is found in an unexpected place. In the sixties, band leader John Mayall deliberately nurtured a number of promising young musicians through his Bluesbreakers Band, giving those musicians pride of place in the line-up and insisting that they continually strove to outperform themselves and him. Without his approach, the careers of musicians such as Peter Green and Eric Clapton might not be where they are today. Contrast this with the de Gaullists who, in 1945, jailed many members of the Maquis who had been fighting for the liberation of France, because to acknowledge their efforts would have been to accept that they had played a more significant role in the liberation than the Free French had from London!

Delegation of tasks and authority

One of the fastest and most effective ways of spreading your power is through the delegation of parts of your job and areas of your decision-making authority. Perhaps it is because it is so effective that many have great difficulty with this process.

There is the old joke about the manager who was told that he was to be sent on a training course on delegation, but as he was so busy, he sent his subordinate in his place. The sad part about the story is that it is probably true! It is therefore necessary to look at the reasons why people are reluctant to delegate. Often the internal dialogue that leads to a non-delegative mind set looks like this:

'I may be busy but I don't want to delegate.'

'Why?'

'Well at the end of the day I am accountable for the work. My head is on the block. Besides, if I do delegate parts of my job, others will not do the work as well as me. They do not understand the implications of its going wrong, yet will still not tell me if it does go wrong.'

Consequently this particular person, if delegating, will spoil it by going into a high command and control mode of management, checking up continually and generally getting in the way. The effect is to demotivate and perhaps even to cause the other person's work to deteriorate. The mind-set therefore continues with the following 'told you so' attitude:

'I'm not surprised, they did not show initiative and I had to unscramble half of what they attempted. Delegation just does not work. Even though I haven't the time, I should have done it all myself.'

One indisputable fact, however, remains. The leader will always retain accountability for the achievement of the task. However, it is also part of the leader's on-going accountability to develop others, to trust and enable them to achieve the objectives as well as if the leader had done it personally.

We are all subject to the golden rule of delegation:

'Nobody should do work that can be done equally well by somebody who is paid less.'

Given then that to delegate is not an option but a necessity, the following *delegation check list* should be a launching pad for future action:

1. Am I working at the right level?

2. Is some of the work I do routine or repetitive?

3. What tasks could I easily delegate?

4. Is there someone to whom these tasks could be delegated?

5. What tasks could I delegate but do not because they are fun? Is this fair?

6. On the other hand am I delegating something because I hate doing it. Is this logical or fair?

7. What areas of my personal authority do I delegate?

8. What is my comfort level here and is it realistic?

9. If I am delegating authority, have I cleared the way with others in authority for this to happen?

10. Can I train or coach so that I can delegate to someone?

11. Is it possible to redesign the job to allow parts of it to be delegated, or given out as projects?

12. Do I feel too busy to plan all this delegation? If so, why?

13. What would happen to the work if I were to fall under the proverbial bus?

The factor that unlocks many of these questions is *coaching*.

Coaching skills

The first thing that has to be defined about coaching is that it is not an option. It is a key demand on leaders and it is one of the ways that a leader leads.

Coaching is the process of helping others to learn more about their jobs in order to improve their performance on those jobs, boost their confidence levels and strengthen their decision-making abilities. There are a number of features of coaching that distinguish it from formal training or the mere issuing of instructions.

Features of coaching

It takes place on the job and uses the person's job tasks as the vehicle for the coaching. Consequently, every time there is a new problem or whenever the member of staff is faced with a demanding task there is an opportunity for coaching.

Coaches recognize that people can learn from everything they do, and must therefore be on the look out for opportunities to coach. This belief that people can and must continually learn should be an underpinning belief in all coaching and must permeate the coach's approach.

During the coaching relationship the coach must spend a lot of time helping the other person, showing or explaining how things are done and encouraging by giving candid feedback mixed with encouragement and praise, where due. In fact, the attitude of the leader during the coaching will do much to shape the attitudes and subsequent behaviour of the person being coached. So, coaching taken too lightly may well result in a cavalier approach to the tasks at a later date.

Opportunities to coach

The opportunities to coach are many but may be so obvious that they could be overlooked:

1. When someone is new in a role. They may in fact be diffident about asking for help but this does not mean that they do not need it.

2. When someone is expanding their responsibilities within an existing role or gearing up for a change in job within your department. The classic case here is when good technicians have a selling role added to their job. Suddenly, although still within their sphere of competence, they are confronted with the challenge of being inexpert.

3. Delegation of tasks or authority is a superb opportunity for coaching. If the area of delegation is significant, then there should be opportunities to plan the coaching session, and to use it to impress the significance of the new duties on the person being coached and to assess that person's attitude.

4. As organizations become increasingly project-based there will be plenty of opportunities to select projects that will stretch people and require them to seek coaching to help them reach successful conclusions. Indeed, more and more formal management training programmes are becoming linked to projects as a means of crystallizing the learning. The use of coaches and mentors is usually a key function of this approach.

5. Finally, when someone appears to be struggling with their work. While the autocrat will look for ways of punishing this person, the leader will initially look for ways of helping—and coaching may be the only remedy.

Steps, skills and attitudes

1. *Look for the opportunity*   The opportunity may well come disguised as a problem: a problem person, a work log jam, or the new project that must be completed.

2. *Plan the session*   How are you going to do it? What materials or papers will be required? When is the best time to coach and will the other person be ready?

3. *Implement the coaching*   There is no one exclusive way to coach, but certain behavioural skills, such as appropriate

questioning, effective listening, and the giving of useful feedback, are vital.

In fact, the skills of giving meaningful feedback as opposed to mere criticism are vital to the success of the coaching. There are a number of essential ground rules. Feedback should always be timely, if it is too late after an event then it will lose its impact. The person giving the feedback should give facts before opinions and use observations based on what has been observed rather than inferences. The most powerful feedback describes things about which the receivers can do something (rather than aspects of their personalities) and promotes understanding of what they are doing or where they are going through reflective questions.

4. *Review progress*   Seldom, if ever, is everything learnt in one session. By its very nature, coaching is an on-going process and therefore progress should be checked and built on in each new session.

5. *Accept challenges*   The other person may well have new ideas about how the job could be done and may suggest changes. Listen to what that person has to say and do not be too quick to demolish suggestions. The idea might just be a good one.

THE HAND-OVER

While some jobs such as sales jobs which often use dual calling as a strategy, lend themselves to coaching and feedback, others are harder.

One situation where a high level of coaching was called for but where both parties initially found the process difficult was in the case of the hand-over of a job from one person to another. A personnel manager in a division of GEC was to retire in two years' time and his successor had been brought in as personnel manager (designate) from another company.

There was a 30-year age gap between the two men and while they liked each other they found communication difficult. The young manager felt the need to prove himself and not be a clone of the older, while the older man could not help feeling some resentment at the younger man's energy and annoyance at what he felt was his 'know-all' attitude. In fact, both felt insecure and wanted a frank discussion although neither knew how to initiate it.

After several months they had jointly to handle a dispute with the unions and the unions fielded an experienced negotiator for the occasion. The young manager asked to lead the negotiation for the company and the older manager reluctantly agreed. Soon the union negotiator began to tie the young manager up in knots and he began to struggle while still trying to preserve a peaceful atmosphere. He was on the ropes and the union negotiator knew it.

Just as he was closing in for the kill the older personnel manager spoke for the first time in several minutes. 'That remark you made then', he said to the union representative, 'I have never heard such rubbish in all my life.' The union man was astounded. 'How can you be so arrogant as to say that?' he spluttered.

'Arrogant? You call me arrogant?' came the reply. 'You come into my business knowing nothing about it and telling me what's good for it. You're the one whose arrogant.' Speechless, the union negotiator left the room.

The older manager turned to his colleague and started to apologize for butting in but was gratified when the younger man thanked him profusely. 'I was totally stuck,' he said 'but it never occurred to fight back in that way.' The older man confessed that was only one way to negotiate and that a confrontational approach was not the ideal learning model, but then asked his colleague what he would do next in order to get the negotiations under way again. A coaching relationship had begun.

In the end the older man volunteered to retire nine months early as he felt that his colleague was more than ready to step into his shoes. Both managers now openly displayed pride that they had worked and coached together for the hand-over.

Coaching—the sad reality

The sad fact is that coaching, despite being one of the most vital ways by which a manager leads, is not used enough. Reasons abound, and range from the fact that many organizations do not appear to value the process and do not give their blessing for quality time to be spent on this activity. Managers themselves may not understand the value of coaching or may secretly lack the confidence to do it. Others may harbour a more negative belief that if they share their expertise with others they may somehow diminish their own expert power base. Whatever the reasons, organizations must appreciate that coaching is the key to success.

In sport, the quality and quantity of coaching is one of the most vital ingredients of success and survival. It may take a definitive act of leadership to change organizational values to a more sporting basis.

Facilitiation

Alan Mumford, one of the world's foremost experts on the learning process, has transferred the objectives and talents of facilitation into an organizational model. He states that organizations facilitate learning when, among others, they:

- Encourage managers to identify their own learning needs.

- Encourage managers to set themselves challenging goals.

- Assist managers in finding learning opportunities on the job.

- Seek to provide new experiences from which managers can learn.

- Encourage them to review what they have done, conclude, and plan further learning activities.

Most important, an organization should regard the extent to which managers develop others as a key performance criterion on which they themselves are reviewed and (once again a clear challenge to style of leadership) it should encourage managers to challenge the traditional ways of doing things.

The learning organization

Much has been written in academic circles about the learning organization, but the expression itself is meaningless and confusing. Organizations themselves cannot learn but the people in them can and, in doing, can transform them. Consequently, it will be the way in which the leaders of organizations encourage learning and the continual development of their people in times of change that will make the difference between success or failure.

The chief executive of Shell stated at the start of the decade: 'The ability to learn *faster* than your competitors may be the only sustainable advantage for the nineties.' However, *what is learning*? Organizations must view their environment and forge a direction based on product, approach, and a shared vision. It is the way and speed with which people learn within the organization that will make the competitive difference here. Effective delegation, coaching, facilitation, and the sharing of power downwards will make all the difference in the *application* of that learning.

Peter Senge has made the distinction between *adaptive* and *generative* learning. Adaptive learning is about coping with the situation, adapting and responding positively to the changing environment. Generative learning is about being creative, about expanding one's ability and actively looking for new solutions.

Building on the Shell view, the ability of an organization to *apply* learning, using both adaptive and generative approaches, may be the only sustainable competitive advantage for the nineties and well beyond. Once again, a challenge to leaders at all levels.

Followership

The extent to which a leader is judged to be successful is very likely to depend on the talents of that leader's followers. The implications of this are that it is the observable effect of the leader's influence on the followers that will prove whether or not that leader is effective. Good leadership will be seen in the way that the followers behave and in the product of their activities. After all, leadership can only be enacted via interaction with other people.

Robert E. Kelly, in the *Harvard Business Review* is one of the few writers to deal in any detail with the concept of followership. This is not surprising, he states, as leadership is a more glamorous concept, yet preoccupation with it prevents us from considering the nature of follower-ship and its importance. This is a pity, as most people spend more of their time being followers than leaders and even leaders need to be followers for some of the time.

Kelly divides followers into five types and differentiates them by their proclivity towards being either passive or active and then by their display of either independent, critical thinking or, on the other hand, dependent, non-critical thinking. In looking at these types of followers it may be possible to recognize traits in those who work for you or even certain traits in yourself.

Sheep

Sheep are distinguished by being passive in approach and dependent and non-critical in their thinking. They are the people who will do what they are told and not question why they have been asked to do it, but yet need supervision because their level of initiative and probably also commitment is low.

Those in the sheep category will be passive and uncritical and lacking initiative and a sense of responsibility. Concepts like total quality manage-ment will be alien to them as their inclination will be to perform the tasks allocated to them and then stop. Most leaders, when faced with sheep will adopt an S1 (highly directive but low in supportive behaviour) approach (See Chapter 1). Unfortunately, although this approach probably gets results in the short term, it will probably reinforce the sheeplike behaviour!

Yes people

The classic picture of the yes person can be seen in the caricature so often found in old movies. This is the person who follows the boss around, tries to anticipate every move, and is always there to light the cigar or to open the door. While most yes-person behaviour is not so overt, elements still remain. This type of behaviour is characterized by an active approach backed by non-independent, non-critical thinking.

If you have yes people working for you, you may feel quite comfortable about it. But are they good for you? Yes behaviour is livelier than sheep behaviour but is unenterprising. The yes person lacks initiative or curtails it and stays dependent on the leader for ideas or inspiration. The yes person will be deferential towards the leader, avoid questioning any decision and may even become servile and fawning. 'Great idea, Boss. Why didn't I think of that?'

While yes people may be flattering to the ego, they represent a threat to the leader in that they will allow the boss to become carried away with plans or ideas. If there are flaws in the leader's approach this type of follower will allow them to develop and may even encourage them. While a good leader should be a catalyst of ideas, followers should represent the crucible in which the ideas are refined. Without the crucible, dangers that can destroy the leader await and it is a sad fact that those in charge who lack confidence or who are lacking in judgement are those most likely to be seduced by the siren call of the yes people.

Alienated followers

These followers are independent in their thinking but very passive in their approach. They are the sort of people who will infuriate a leader as there is always the suspicion that more could be given, but is not. At best these people will simply not act up to their potential; at worst they will become a focus for grumbling, unrest, and silent rebellion.

Kelly guesses that somewhere along the line, someone or something turned these people off. Was it a major disappointment? Were they overlooked? Do they feel that, given their qualifications, they should be more senior? Whatever the case, these people are not choosing to give the leader all their energy and commitment. Their approach will be a mixture of cynicism and passivity. Tasks will be done passively and with surly acquiescence. Although alienated followers may have thought of good alternative approaches, they will seldom bother to share them with the leader.

Sadly, there are many thousands of people who fall into this category, and it is tragic that so many are young. The sensitive leader should regard this category as the biggest challenge. You should ask what it is that you may have done to bring about this sort of behaviour, what it is about the organization and, most of all, what you could do to bring about a change in this attitude.

Survivors

We have all met survivors. They are the people who seem to sail through countless reorganizations and always be around. They do this by perpetually 'testing the wind' and by adapting their behaviour to suit what they see as the prevailing tide of events. They know when to adopt active or passive approaches and they know when to keep their heads down.

The main problem with survivors is that they will put survival before initiative and their main preoccupation will be with looking after themselves rather than assessing their potential contribution.

Effective followers

The first thing that strikes one about truly effective followers is their similarity to leaders. They are characterized by an active approach, coupled to independent and critical thinking.

If you have effective followers you will know it. They will tell you what they think of your ideas and bombard you with their own. When allocated work they will carry it out with energy and initiative, seeking to solve problems independently and to take calculated risks where appropriate. They are the sort of person that the good leader likes to have on the team.

Effective followers will display commitment to the organization and to the task in hand. They will also try to develop themselves in order to grow their competence and be able to focus their efforts for the most impact.

When you consider that you have effective followers, nurture them, adapt your style to theirs, and encourage their efforts while giving the level of support that you consider to be appropriate. If the followers are already skilled in the work, try S3, the low directive style, that still offers support when needed.

Making the most of your followers

If followers *do* make good leaders good then it is certainly your responsibility, if not plain self-interest, to be aware of the types of follower you have and to use them in a way that helps both them and you to be more effective. If, for example, you judge your followers to be sheep, is there anything that can be done about it? Is it just them or have you inherited them from someone who did not require anything more? Can they be snapped out of their sheeplike approach? Would they respond to a challenge? Whatever your initial impressions, do not give up too easily.

Yes people present a different threat. It is all too easy to bask in the ego-building atmosphere that these people create. The answer is simple. Do not reward this form of behaviour. Be 'hard to please' and give credit only where it is really due.

The alienated present a challenge as well as a threat. Why are they this way? Once again, if they are inherited, what has gone on before? It may be necessary to ask a lot of questions, to have a heart to heart with them or, if that fails, to issue challenges, repeat your vision and encourage debate around it.

Survivors are an enigma. If they have been successful in surviving, can the energy and ingenuity they have put into survival be channelled into something more purposeful and directional such as the overall objective? As insecurity may underpin their behaviour they may need considerable reassurance and the certainty that you are to be trusted.

Developing effective followers into leaders

The development of any follower is a positive act of leadership and the development of already effective followers is a mature act requiring a sophisticated approach. The following thoughts are applicable to the development of most followers, but particularly those who are already effective and showing initiative:

1. Do not be afraid of them. Giving power to others will not necessarily diminish your power base.

2. Give challenging assignments and show trust in their ability to cope.

3. Allow them to take on leadership roles of their own. Is there a task, assignment, or project they can champion?

4. Find their views and ask questions which release their creative intelligence. Then listen intently and with respect.

5. Help them through difficulties, giving both praise and assistance when due.

6. Give them the benefit of honest but useful feedback and allow them to give you feedback in return.

These are all steps towards *transformational leadership*, the talent for being able to rise above mere task focuss towards a form of leadership that is both truly inspiring and truly infectious.

Transformational leadership

In being both inspiring and infectious, transformational leadership is not so much a method of leading as an attitude of mind on the leader's behalf that changes the leader, the followers, and also the situation. This attitude of mind shows itself in a number of ways. Warren Bennis said that 'managers do things right but leaders do the right thing' and this can be seen in a number of things that the leader chooses to do, or be:

1. *An initiator and influencer*   The leader takes time to develop a vision and uses it to respond to change positively, in fact, to look for ways of making change happen. As part of this the leader will seek to gain the trust and confidence of other people, making sure that the team shares the vision and sense of common purpose.

2. *Inspirational*   To be inspirational does not mean going on a

prolonged ego trip but means seeking to increase the enthusiasm and optimism of the followers, making them as effective and individually powerful as can be. This may mean that you seek out every opportunity to reiterate the vision in a way that is meaningful to others and, at times, choosing to be more forthright or extrovert than may come naturally.

3. *Challenging and stimulating*   This is closely allied to being inspirational but is about *applied* inspiration. The challenging leader asks followers to be creative and leads from the front in this respect by questioning old approaches. This leader also stimulates others by deliberately taking a different approach to problem-solving. If a logical approach has failed in the past, why continue with it? Can we use our intuition and then back it by logic? This leader will encourage brainstorming as a method of working and will challenge others to throw in their ideas and to give their colleagues the benefit of their unique experience. It will be *fun* to work for this leader!

4. *Understanding followers' needs*   While being stimulating yet probably still hard to please, this leader will be considerate of the needs of the followers. Tasks will be delegated and coaching, advice, praise, and feedback will follow as a matter of course. The leader will be both a catalyst for change and a booster of people's confidence when the time comes for its implementation. A particular feature of this leader's approach is that, while retaining a mental toughness, a high level of approachability will remain.

Summary

Much of the remainder of this book will be involved with the development of the talents, skills, and attitudes that make a transformational leader. Some parts, such as the chapter on visions, already fall within this arena. Certainly, it is difficult to separate the concept of transformational leadership from more generalized discussions on 'effective leadership' as so much of the behaviour required in the latter part of the 20th century *must* be transformational in approach in order to be effective.

The concept of deliberately giving away power may not come easily, but it is a crucial theme in the development of a leader. For those who fear giving up a command and control style, it is worth stating that empowerment does not mean giving up control altogether, but does mean changing the way in which it is exercised. If the leader leads by communicating the vision or big picture, and then generates commitment and enthusiasm by showing others their roles in attaining the vision, it is only a small step towards the followers developing the skills and creativity that will enable the common goal to be reached.

Your WIFMs from this chapter

- How do you feel about power, especially about giving it to others?
- Do you delegate as often and as well as you might?
- Have you analysed the situations and ways that you could coach your people?
- Into what category do your followers fall, and why?
- How would you rate yourself as a follower?
- How often do you actively attempt to challenge (or even inspire!) other people to achieve greater things?

Leadership and change

There is a clock at the Pompidou Centre in Paris that is like no other. It subtracts seconds and so appears to be counting backwards. This in itself sounds ridiculous. From what is it counting backwards and towards what is it subtracting? The answer is that it is counting the seconds to the year 2000. As the millenium finally arrives it will, in turn, reach zero.

Of course the seconds to the millenium number many million but if you visit the Pompidou Centre look at the clock with its long array of decreasing digits and then take some time going around the attractions within the centre or, alternatively, buy an ice cream and pass an enjoyable period listening to the local street musicians before returning to look at the clock. You will find the display of digits significantly altered. Time has moved on and more than digits will have changed during that period.

Like it or not, the future is approaching fast, and if we approach it as mature leaders it is ours for both the making and the taking. By the same token, if leadership is concerned with making change happen, then the way in which you approach it will be a governing factor in whether or not you are successful.

The pace of change

A definition of history could be that it is the story of change. If this definition is true (and I prefer it to other definitions such as the Marxist version which defines it as the story of class conflict) then the story is speeding up. It has always been an exciting story, but now more is crammed onto each page; the time between events is shortening, it is becoming harder to predict what will be found on the following page.

Probably the greatest instigator of change is the technology that permeates every corner of our personal and professional lives. Information is available faster and in greater quantity than ever before. It hits us via the media which bombard us with challenges to accepted attitudes and values, and its usage alters the very way in which we work. Fall behind the challenges of the technology and risk being branded as a dinosaur!

Events move with staggering pace and catch most of us unawares. Two weeks before the fall of the Berlin Wall you could have placed a bet with odds of over ten to one with London bookmakers that it would not be dismantled in the 20th century. Who would have guessed that the world would be looking at another institutionalized racial persecution within Europe only a few decades after the horrors of the Nazi holocaust? Similarly, values are changing, and attitudes to homosexuality, marriage, race, religion, the federalization of Europe, and the British monarchy are all vastly different from what they were just a few short years ago.

If all of this seems unnerving then there is little comfort ahead if you are determined not to espouse change. Charles Handy in *The Age of Unreason*, debatably one of the best insights into the probable effects of future changes on both individuals and organizations, wrote:

> We are entering an age of unreason, a time when the future, in so many areas, is to be shaped by us and for us; a time when the only prediction that will hold true is that no prediction will hold true; a time therefore, for bold imaginings in private life as well as public, for thinking the unlikely and doing the unreasonable.

A PERSONAL REFLECTION

Handy makes a telling point that at the start of his career he joined a multinational company and was informed that his future had been mapped out for him. If he performed as expected he would at the end of his career be in a given job in a certain subsidiary organization in a certain country. He now looked back to see that not only did the job no longer exist but neither did the subsidiary organization nor the country in which it had been based.

While writing this book I visited one of my organization's clients near Manchester. I arrived early for the appointment and found that I had time to have lunch in Wilmslow where my first head office had been based. The organization no longer existed, that I already knew, but I was astounded to find that the office block in which it had been situated had been demolished and half the street was now engulfed by new roundabouts.

I then reflected that like Charles Handy I was not in my original occupation but, more significantly, five of the seven organizations I had worked for now no longer existed or no longer existed as separate entities!

Not all the changes that take place will appear right, just, or logical to those affected by them. Certainly, change by no means benefits everybody and there will be those who feel considerably threatened by events which appear very minor to others. This is where leadership is called for. Probably the greatest test of leadership

at any level is in the ways that the leader helps other people to accept change
and then the ways that the change itself is implemented. It therefore makes sense
to continue by looking at change through the eyes of those who are affected
by it.

Why people resist change

Of course, not everybody does resist change and if you think about it, life
itself is all about change and is a continuing change process. However,
there is a presumption by many that change is something to be feared, that
the likelihood of its bringing benefits is vastly outweighed by the probability of its bringing disadvantages, if not disaster.

One thing is certain, however, and that is that people react strongly to
change, whether it be favourably or negatively, and therefore it is important
to examine the reasons why this strength of reaction may exist. Rather
than looking at an emotive subject too academically, it is better to examine
it through a process of personal reflection.

Think of a time or situation where you felt reluctant to change, or
accept the changes that were happening. What was going on in your mind,
and why? Then, think of a time when you felt good about a changing
situation. Once again, what was going on in your mind, and why?

The probability is that when you felt reluctant about the change it was
due to one or more of the following reasons or emotions:

- Felt 'left in the dark'

- Felt unconsulted about the change

- Felt threatened, a pawn in the game

- Did not understand what was going on

- Considered there to be better alternatives or that the change was
  unnecessary

Alternatively, you may simply feel that most change brings about a worse
situation than that which existed previously and that it is therefore
necessary to fight to preserve the status quo before all the good in it is
swept away.

Similarly, when you welcomed change it was probably because you:

- Understood why it was necessary

- Saw the potential benefits

- Felt that there were opportunities to be grasped

- Considered the change to be inevitable but felt that you had some influence over what the final situation would be

- Had instigated the change yourself or were an active member of the change implementation team

On the other hand, you may regard change as constant and necessary, as a process that provides constant opportunities that must be grasped in the most effective way possible.

The important thing to note is that many of the reactions to change, especially the negative reactions, are emotional and based around feelings. The positive reactions, while still retaining an element of emotion, tend to be more logical and factually based.

A common feature of the favourable reactions to change is the underlying assumption that the individual has some ability to influence and determine the outcome of events or at least knows and understands *why* they are taking place. Perhaps this fact explains much about why people react to change in different ways. Change, after all, is a constant factor in all of our lives. The very art of living is about change and without it we are dead.

Through childhood, into adolescence, into adulthood, and then old age, we undergo a process of change. As we mature we not only go through physical changes but also take more control over the events and changes in our own lives. We decide which course of study to follow, whom to marry, when to change job, what friends to have, when to move house, when to redecorate, etc. If we then consider that there are only 25 567 days in a lifetime of 70 years, it can be seen that changes come at us thick and fast. While we are in control of events we will probably welcome and initiate changes in our lives, as this is part of being adult. When we lose control of the events and changes in our lives however, we are far less likely to welcome the changes. Have we forcibly been put into the role of child and is the emotional reaction consequently a logical and understandable one?

Consequences of change in organizations

As in life, change is a constant factor within all organizations and it is interesting to note that the more negative consequences of organizational change bite deeply at an emotional level and often have the effect of forcing responsible adults into roles that conflict with their perceptions of themselves as mature individuals. They are forced into a child role! Therein lies both the challenge and the trap for the leader. A consideration of some of the individual consequences of change in organizations should illustrate why change itself is often feared and resisted.

Loss of control

When there is a degree of stability people tend to work out the parameters of their situation. Within their jobs they know what and whom they control. They also understand who else controls important factors within the organization—and to what extent. The power structure is relatively stable and there is comfort to be derived from that fact.

When the organization enters a period of rapid or significant change, the comfortable status quo is threatened. Often a period of change can be accompanied by a tightening of control measures within the organization while new methods of operation are bedded down, and thus the change is perceived as an erosion of the individual's power, status, or control of procedures and people. As many changes alter departmental boundaries or 'rationalize' numbers (in both budgetary and human terms) there is usually truth in the plaintive cry that: 'Once I had control over events but now that seems to have passed to others.'

Loss of face

Coupled to the loss of control is loss of face. When organizations change there are inevitably winners and losers. Old power bases wane and new ones rise as the comparative importance of functions and people change to meet the demands of new markets, new technology, or different clients.

Sometimes the changes mean redundancy for some, but often they simply alter the balance of power and status. Organization charts, those dry descriptors of level and function, alter and in so doing can silently point to massive dents to individuals' pride and self-esteem as responsibilities disappear or move from one person to another.

It can be that whereas redundancy is a painful shock (yet sometimes the much-needed start to a new and better life), the loss of face associated with 'losing out' in the reshuffle of change can be the equivalent to the death of a thousand cuts as the 'loser' struggles to cope with the new status and the new image in the mind of others.

THE NON-JOB

The cruellest example of 'a thousand cuts' came after a reorganization to meet new client pressures within the defence industry. An electronics company had been selling on a project basis to the Army and Royal Navy at 'cost plus'! At the end of the project the costs of delivering the project were totalled, the agreed profit margin added, and the final invoice submitted. This was fine for the supplier as profit was guaranteed, but not so fine for the taxpayer!

A move away from this method of doing business towards contracts with other commercial organizations who insisted that projects were delivered according to previously agreed costs meant a major overhaul in the way the electronics company organized itself. The major casualty was a general manager who had previously had responsibility for hundreds of people, two factories and multimillion pound contracts. He suddenly found himself as director in charge of staff requisitions, which meant that now his only responsibility was for approving the requisition of new or replacement staff against a budget that somebody else had set.

Whether he was given this job out of misplaced kindness ('Well, its better than firing him.') or overt cynicism ('It would be expensive to fire him so let's make his life so unbearable that he leaves, anyway.') never became clear. What was painfully clear, however, was that the loss of face was progressively destroying him. In the months before he finally left he seldom left his (smaller) office, did not speak to anybody, and sat alone in the dining room. It was certainly a fate worse than redundancy and one that many other managers feared!

Growth in level of uncertainty

The saying goes that 'there is nothing so powerful as the idea whose time has come'. However, although the idea may be powerful, the means of achieving it may be less certain and high levels of uncertainty or ambiguity may prevail as the idea forces itself into existence.

Although a certain level of uncertainty is stimulating and can inspire creativity, it can rise too high and start to strangle initiative and decision-making. If the options are suddenly too numerous, if the rules of the game are all at once unclear, or if the distinction between what behaviour is rewarded or frowned upon becomes clouded, then it is small wonder that people find it difficult to cope and may opt for inaction rather than action.

Increased political game-playing

Change and the uncertainty that goes with it often have the effect of increasing the level of 'political' activity within an organization. The 'rules' may appear to be suspended and new opportunities open to be grabbed by the adventurous or the manipulative. Change can give opportunities for the settlement of old scores. Words can be dropped into people's ears that Peter or Jane 'just don't seem to be in line with what's going on' or 'don't seem to understand the need to do things differently these days'.

Often it is those of the more conservative disposition who appear to be holding on to the old despite everything, or those who place a very high value on trust and the value of interpersonal relationships who are the most frequent victims in political battles. In all events, when the level of 'politicking' is high everybody, including those who are leading the games, is at the heightened level of alertness or weariness—both can be very tiring because, of course, the imagined threat very often turns out to be real!

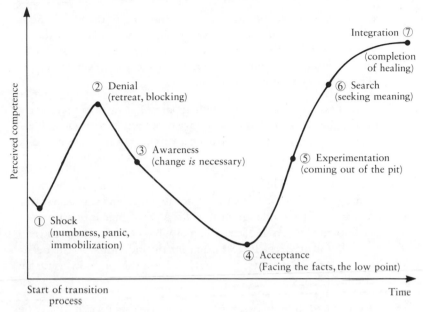

Figure 8.1   The transition curve.

Effects of extreme change on the individual

Any one of the effects of change in an organization can, as illustrated, have a marked effect on the individual; sometimes the effect can be traumatic. It is therefore necessary for the leader to understand more fully the effects of change and trauma on individuals. While the leader may, by introducing changes, have caused the trauma, it is also clearly up to the leader to understand the *effects* of the trauma and to help others through it if the change is to be successful.

The effects of extreme change have been charted in what is known as *the transition curve* (Figure 8.1) This curve, which originated in psychiatry, measures the individual's ability to cope over time after having been hit by sudden or traumatic change. The curve rises and falls as the individual struggles to find a way of adjusting to the change and a closer look at the stages may hint to a sensitive leader what the best intervention may be:

1. *Shock*   This is often felt physically like a blow, quickly followed by numbness or panic. Often the individual may be totally immobilized and may require physical help.

2. *Denial*   A very human reaction. 'Try to pretend it never happened and then maybe it will go away.' This blocking out is a retreat from reality and as such is a coping mechanism. It can be

seen in cases of the recently bereaved referring to the loved one as if he or she were still alive, or sometimes laying a place for the loved one at the table, as if it had never happened. The effect of this 'blocking' is temporarily to raise the individual's perceived ability to cope with the situation.

3. *Awareness*   Here the individual painfully starts to realize that the change is unavoidable, necessary or, at any rate, undeniable. This is accompanied by a growing awareness that it is going to be difficult to cope.

4. *Acceptance*   This is where the new reality really hits home. Things are *not* going to be the same any more and it is necessary to face that fact and let go of the old. As this stage is not always accompanied by an understanding of what can take the place of the old, it is often the lowest point for the individual or the peak of the grief—all pretence is gone. It is from this pit, however, that rebuilding can start.

5/6. *Experimentation and search*   These two stages can follow on closely from one another. From the pit, the individual starts to try out new things. 'If the past is irretrievably gone, what can take its place? What can be tested out?' As new approaches, methods of doing things, or new relationships are tested out the individual seeks meaning from them. This can lead to a better understanding of self and a realization that change is possible and perhaps even desirable.

7. *Integration*   The healing is complete. The individual now behaves differently, has changed values and is actively operating in a different way. When integration is really successful the individual may sometimes wonder how it was that things were ever different.

REDUNDANT AGAIN!

Graham, a good friend of mine, worked in the insurance industry, allied to Lloyd's. As a senior member of the syndicate, he was one of the first to go.

Although shocked, Graham was philosophical about his redundancy. These things happen in life and he decided to put himself on the job market with a great deal of energy. He wrote a large number of applications, visited recruitment consultants, and put his house on the market in case a move was called for. Within three months his efforts had paid off and he was offered a good job, still in insurance, but in a different line and therefore in a different part of the country. It meant moving house but it was worth it.

Within a year the axe fell again. Graham had barely moved his family into the new area and this time he was shattered. He telephoned me the same day that he got the news and he had virtually lost his voice from shock.

We met several times over the next few weeks and I was surprised at the way he wanted to talk about work and the way he referred to his own job as if he still had it. It was as if, by talking about work this way, he was trying to convince himself, as well as others, that he was still a 'working man'.

Once again, his house went on the market and was sold. Graham and his family went into rented accommodation and it was then that depression really struck. The old props of job and home ownership were gone and he started to denigrate himself, saying that they were probably right to let him go. It was only when he came to the conclusion that there was nothing wrong with him as a person, but that after his earlier experiences he had no wish to be someone else's employee again, that he began to change.

In accepting that he did not want to work for other people and that there was consequently no point in sending off job applications, he was forced to ask himself what he was going to do for the rest of his working life. Slowly an old ambition reawakened, that of self-employment, running a small hotel. When he accepted that this was what he *did* want to do he quickly channelled his considerable energies into raising money, surveying properties, and finally making the purchase.

Graham and his family opened the hotel just in time to face the worst recession in Britain since the Second World War. Undeterred, they fought on with Graham using all his sales skills and business acumen to work for himself. Looking back, now he is one of the few people who can truly say, 'Recession? What recession?'

The role of the leader

The fact that organizations create change and that change can be traumatic for individuals places a number of responsibilities on leaders at all levels. If many of the extreme reactions to change stem from feelings of powerlessness or lack of understanding, then it is up to you as leader to *give meaning* to the changes which will unlock people's ability to cope and be powerful within the situation. Giving meaning in itself is a fairly meaningless expression so to make it real, I have divided the concept into the following implications for a leader:

- Understanding the role of the leader as a change agent

- Being sensitive to the reactions of other people

- Having a mental model of how best to 'sell' change

- Knowing the qualities demanded of oneself to see it through

The rest of this chapter will be devoted to an examination of these core leadership competencies and their implications for you as a leader.

The leader as change agent

Do you allow the future to come to meet you or do you go out to meet the future as it arrives and, in so doing, influence the shape it will take? In *On Becoming a Leader*, Warren Bennis states that leaders must 'forge the future', in other words to be a leader is to take influence over events and to mould them to your vision. This may sound realizable only at chief executive level but, in practice, this need not be the case as the successful leader should empower others to forge that piece of their future, or operation, over which they have control. The chief roles after that will be of the coordination of the individual energies towards the realization of the greater goal. How is this done?

First of all the leader must understand the concept of the *arithmetic of change*. This is quite simple and really means that *if there is a general dissatisfaction with the way things are and if this dissatisfaction is coupled to a recognition that certain other things are both desirable and achievable, you have the right conditions for change to take place.* Behind this formula there is the need for both persuasion and a cool assessment of the prevailing climate, something that the good listener will find easier to achieve than the autocrat.

A structured approach to making the arithmetic of change work for you might work along the following lines:

1. *Assess the readiness*   Speak to people, listen a lot, intuit the nature of their WIFMs. Ascertain their worries, find out what they dislike about the status quo—it might prove to be a powerful lever.

2. *Build commitment*   Who are the potential allies? Continue to sell the benefits and stress your commitment and belief in the change. Think in terms of a critical mass; once 20 per cent of those involved are committed to the change, the snowball will start rolling downhill and gather momentum. So, think of the crucial few and think of the apostolic theory. Sometimes the appointment of just one or two champions, people whose future success is closely linked to the achievement of the objectives, is all that is needed.

3. *Introduce the change*   Whatever it is, it should be done efficiently. This is where good management as well as good leadership must prevail. If mistakes occur then the sceptics will say 'I told you so!'; do not give them the chance, but at the same time support those who may be finding the adjustment difficult. Guess where they may be on the transition curve. What kind of reassurance may they need from you?

4. *Integrate the change*   First of all, accept that people often need a

chance to 'mourn the past.' This may take the form of eulogizing about how good the previous situation was with a degree of nostalgia. This is only natural and is often most prevalent when a change of location is involved. However, the job is to move them through this into accepting and integrating the changes, whether they be organizational or skills based, into their everyday behaviour. In other words, you must bring those involved out to stage 7 of the curve. This can be done by praising effort and rewarding the desired behaviour.

More powerfully, it can be done by constantly reiterating the purpose and meaning of the changes by illustrating the realized benefits whenever possible. Do not take it for granted that others will be as quick to see the benefits as you, so do not worry about appearing to overemphasize the meaning behind what is occurring.

To help you further to manage your way through the preceding four stages, the following questions to ask yourself when planning change should prove to be a useful checklist:

1. Why do you think change is required?

2. What do you really want to see happen? Is your vision clear? How will you express it to give meaning to others?

3. How will you make the change happen? How will you set out to influence people or events?

4. What are your goals and how will you know whether they have been achieved?

5. Who will oppose you? How powerful are they?

6. Who will support you? How powerful are they and what resources do they have?

7. What additional information do you need and who has access to it?

8. If your first choice of action fails do you have any alternative plans to be implemented?

9. How will you consolidate the new position once it is reached and ensure its integration into future behaviour?

10. Finally, once you have achieved the change, how confident are you that you will not be the opponent of further changes or new ideas?

The process of working your way through the above checklist should help you decide whether you are ready personally as well as organizationally to take on the role of change agent. Organizations need to be fit and healthy, with channels of communication as well as feedback when change is proposed. Similarly, the individuals need to be 'in good shape', as implementing change will impose challenges of conflict and interpersonal sensitivity as dreams struggle to become reality. It is therefore necessary to examine your behaviour as change agent in the light of the potential reactions of other people and the pressures and conflict that this can provoke.

The reactions of other people

All around us there are opposing forces. The Marxist conflict theory of history simplifies everything that has gone before into the battle for resources and generators of wealth between those who own them and those who do not. Within the individual there are also a number of forces, or drives. It is these drives, given certain stimuli, that make us behave the way we do.

A large number of psychological models exist to explain behaviour and the reactions to stimuli and it is not the intention here to review them. There is one model, however, that goes a long way to explain the opposing forces within us and how they alter in their degree of influence on both attitude and behaviour according to pressures placed upon the individual. As change is one of the prime causes of pressure, this is an ideal model for explaining what may appear to be the irrational reactions of many to the pressures of change

The LIFO® model

Katcher and Atkins have designed an approach based on people's Life Orientations (LIFO®). Unlike most models of behaviour it does not categorize or type people but emphasizes that the range of human behaviour is available to all of us but that many people feel comfortable with only a part of that range. We can use our behavioural pattern productively, even if the range is limited. We can also use it unproductively by relying on it too much, a proposition which will be further explored in Chapter 9.

Perhaps the most significant contribution of the LIFO model is that it recognizes that behaviour can change when an individual is under pressure or feels threatened. Consequently, it provides a useful basis on which to analyse people's personal reactions to change. If people feel threatened by change, often the behaviour they adopt to cope with the threat results in their exaggerating the reliance on some of their behavioural characteristics. This is likely to produce behaviour inappropriate to the situation they find themselves in. Some people's behavioural characteristics alter so dramatically that the behaviour we normally see when they feel comfortable is no longer displayed and is replaced by a different pattern of behaviour, giving rise to different reactions and a totally new approach to handling situations.

The LIFO model identifies four behavioural approaches to people and events, each of which has a positive and a negative side. To help you understand your reactions to change it is necessary to examine each in turn.

1. Supporting/giving-in behaviour

When someone uses this orientation they espouse the following philosophy to a greater or lesser extent. 'If I am responsive to others, pursue excellence and follow my ideals, my conscientiousness will be appreciated and rewarded without asking.' Behind this are some specific personal goals:

- to be seen as a responsive and worthy person

- to feel valued, understood, accepted and trusted

- to feel that their ideals are not sacrificed.

- having an inclination to work with others, add value and protect others from harm.

Consequently when using the supporter/giver-in orientation, a person wants to be seen by others as supportive, considerate, idealistic, modest, helpful, responsive, cooperative and seeking excellence. If we use these strengths in the appropriate situation most people will react positively to us. They are valuable strengths that can facilitate change. If, however, we overdo them, then others will see self-denying, self-effacing, passive, gullible, overcommitted, perfectionist or compliant behaviour. In other words, weaknesses. Some may wish to take advantage of these weaknesses while others may simply find them irritating. These weaknesses can adversely affect the change process by removing discernment, stifling individual initiative and encouraging 'group think'.

2. Controlling/taking over behaviour

When someone uses this orientation, the approach can be summed up thus: 'If I want things to happen, I have to make them happen and convince people of my competence.' The personal goals behind this orientation are:

- to be seen as powerful, capable and competent

- to feel able to overcome all obstacles

- to feel that there are still opportunities to be seized

- having a wish to accept challenges and have focused objectives.

When using this orientation a person wants to be seen by others to be self-confident, quick to act, challenging, directing, forceful, change-seeking, urgent, risk-taking and competitive. All of these qualities are useful in times of change and especially when things need to be accomplished. If we use these strengths in the appropriate situation, most people will react positively to us. These are the strengths that supply initiative and the willingness to take on challenges which help most change processes. If we overdo them, however, others will see domineering, arrogant, impulsive, coercive, impatient, gambling, impatient or even inquisitorial behaviour. So the strengths essential to making change happen have become weak-nesses that are likely to make people perceive the change as a far greater threat than it actually is, or can cause the process to go out of control.

3. Conserving/Holding-on behaviour

If the controller/taker can become the irresistible force, the conserver/holder might be seen as the immovable object by virtue of the behaviour adopted. The essential orientation could be described as: 'I have to preserve what I have and use existing resources to build the future on the past in a careful and rational way.'

The personal goals that support this orientation are:

- to be seen as objective, purposeful and rational

- to feel able to minimize and eliminate risks

- to feel that no loss is irreparable

- having to wish to get the most out of a given investment.

Consequently the person adopting this behaviour may be seen by others as tenacious, practical, cost-conscious, steadfast, prudent, thorough, reserved and analytical. However those with different orientations, especially those of controlling/taking may find this behaviour irritating and especially so when the strengths are over used. It is then that the behaviour moves into *holding* and then will be perceived as clinging, unimaginative, mean, data-bound, stubborn, pedantic, plodding, cautious or nit-picking.

Conserving/holding behaviour in excess can do a great deal to slow down or even totally frustrate a change initiative as people displaying this orientation can be as forceful as controller /takers, albeit in a different way and the loggerheads meeting of the two orientations in times of change is often the root cause of much of the conflict that is associated with it.

4. Adapting/dealing-away behaviour

This orientation is different again. The person adopting its driving orientation could be described as follows. 'I have to get on with people and to be sensitive to their needs, then I can set my objectives and plan to achieve them through harmonious cooperation with others.' Underlying this, are the following personal goals:

- to be seen as likeable and popular

- to have everyone feel happy about outcomes

- to feel that there is still a chance to please people.

- to be flexible, not to feel locked onto any specific course of action. To go around difficulties rather than through them.

In adapting, the person favouring this approach may exhibit the following strengths. They may be seen as flexible, experimental, sociable, enthusiastic, tactful, adaptable, with good negotiating skills and socially adept. These are all useful attributes for facilitating the process of change. However, under pressure the behaviour may change from adapting to *dealing away*.

At this stage it may be perceived as inconsistent, aimless, parasitical, fervent, appeasing, convictionless, manipulative or compromising. None of these are the qualities that will enable change management to proceed with any purpose or direction.

Using the LIFO® model to facilitate change through people

Change can be achieved autocratically, by decree, or democratically by bringing people's hearts and minds with you. The latter option may be slower but is likely to be the more effective and longer lasting. In order to move hearts and minds it is necessary to be able to look into them or at least to guess what may be there. This is where the LIFO model of behaviour is so useful and it is worth listing the ways in which a leader can use the framework to achieve change in a more effective, yet sensitive fashion.

- *Use it to estimate where the other person is coming from*   Can what may have previously been regarded as bizarre behaviour now be explainable and can you adjust your approach to achieve a greater degree of empathy? Table 8.1 shows a variety of approaches for dealing with difficult people using an understanding of their main orientations.

- *Look for the causes of the negative*   Appreciate how people's behaviour can cause other people to react negatively and to exaggerate or change drastically their own behaviour. Can opposing parties be brought together to discuss their differences in a non-threatening way?

- *Use a knowledge of your team's orientation to assess its potential strengths in handling change*   All the orientations have their place, the supporting strengths provide the selfless contribution to the general good. Controlling strengths incline to get things done, while conserving strengths ensure that progress is rational and never foolhardy or wasteful. Adapting strengths promote interpersonal harmony and an inclination to look for new angles that may be invisible to others.

- *Use the LIFO language to promote feedback in all directions* Talking about behaviour, using it as a form of shorthand, is far less threatening than attacking personalities.

- *Select the right sort of change champion*   What does the situation demand? Does it require a pusher, a negotiator or a cautious approach— and how is the change champion likely to react when under pressure?

A full appreciation of the LIFO model and its usefulness in both change and conflict management is best obtained by completing the LIFO question- naire and asking members of your team to do so as well. However, the categories of behaviour it deals with are universal and easily recognized so the insights that a knowledge of them can give are applicable even without the more detailed insight that completion of the questionnaire will provide.

The mental model

As the ability to manage change increasingly becomes a core competency, the need for methods and checklists for ensuring that it is managed well increases. Of course, the ability to cope as well as manage in a changing environment is a requirement for more than just the leader. In *The Career Management Challenge*, Peter Herriot argues that a high value should be placed on people's 'responsiveness to change; risk and innovation; tolera- tion of failures; development of people; supportive teamwork'.

He states that underlying key assumptions are that: 'people can change; people can like change; people need help; people help each other; the organization is there to support people'.

Table 8.1 How to deal with the 'difficult' person

	If this is the other person's orientation:			
	Supporting/giving-in	Controlling/taking-over	Conserving/holding-on	Adapting/dealing-away
	Provide support, reassurance and encouragement, don't 'nag'	Try to respond quickly to what they want from you	Try to reduce threat or risk	Reassure them that they really are 'one of us'
	Hear them out—provide listening time	Offer solutions—don't bring up new problems	Do not get emotional	Be willing to try other ways round the problem
	Share some insights relevant to their anxiety, complaint or concern	Be open and firm but confident about your own position	Refer to precedents and link those to successful outcomes	Suggest that you admire people who are open about differences
	Acknowledge the value of their intentions even if the consequences weren't as they desired	Ask questions to help this person feel he/she found their own solution	Invite their suggestions as to criteria that might be used to evaluate problems	Spend some time socializing before pressing for decisions
	Suggest some way they can 'make up' or atone	Suggest some other ways to reach the same objectives	Allow for some cool-off time or delay in decision-making; don't force the issue	Allow them to save face
		Don't make any demands on them	Give some additional facts that the person will accept	
The needs are . . .	To be seen as a responsible and worthwhile person	To be seen as powerful, capable, active and competent	To be seen as objective, rational and careful of resources	To be seen as likeable and flexible
	To feel valued, understood, accepted, trusted by others	To feel able to overcome obstacles	To feel able to minimize or eliminate risks	To have everyone feel happy about outcomes
	To feel that their ideals are not sacrificed	To feel there are still other opportunities to be seized	To feel no loss is irreparable	To feel there is still a chance to please people

Source: © Alan Katcher International Inc.

Herriot states that there is a balancing act between the organization's right to expect loyalty and commitment and people's need to be treated as individuals with rights of their own. The underpinning assumptions here are that people like to know where they stand and also to make sense of their organization.

If we pursue Herriot's line of thought then it becomes clear that one of the greatest challenges to leaders in times of change is the challenge of *unlocking* attitudes and competencies that are probably already there. But how can this be done?

One of the best unlocking mechanisms is the *PACE* model, as described by John Nicholls in his article 'Meta leadership in organizations: applying Burn's political concept in transforming leadership'. This is simple, effective and gives the leader a powerful motivational springboard.

P   *Perception*   What is your perception of the environment and the changes that are taking place? Have you been up in your helicopter and taken an objective overview of what is happening? Can you now see the advantages of the changes?

A   *Articulation*   The perception must be put into words, must be articulated. Can you phrase your understanding of the situation in a way that will unlock understanding in others? Analysis, preparation, and rehearsal may be necessary here.

C   *Conviction*   If your understanding is not conveyed with conviction then it will not motivate. Your understanding should breed enthusiasm within you. If that enthusiasm is there, convey it in the words you use and in your tone of voice.

E   *Empathy*   Without empathy, conviction may come across as 'sounding brass' or as 'full of sound and fury. Signifying nothing!' Think of the other person's WIFMs, or of their probable fears. How can your message alleviate these concerns? Does the other person exhibit a great deal of conserver/holder behaviour? If so, what sort of language will reassure?

The qualities demanded of the leader

Many of the qualities demanded in times of change are the same as those demanded at all times. They are, however, accentuated.

In Chapter 2, the concept of WIST was introduced as a mixture of standards and attitudes that a leader must attain to be effective. The elements of WIST still apply but can now be redefined into three strong forces, each of which must be balanced by a counterforce to prevent its becoming excessive. The combination of balanced forces then becomes a powerful source of strength within you as a leader.

The key forces are those of passion, hardiness, and perseverance, while the three counterbalances are the qualities of compassion, humility, and patience. As can be seen, the balances do not defuse any of the driving forces but in fact turn them from forces into true strengths.

Passion and compassion

In order to make change happen it is necessary to have passion, which could be defined as a dedicated, communicated belief—a conviction that will inspire others. It is so easy, however, for the passion to become intolerance—for the conviction to make the leader forget that there are *people* involved in the equation. To retain compassion to balance the passion means that other individuals' attitudes, fears, and expectations are acknowledged and form part of the equation. This does not mean that tough decisions no longer need be made, but it does mean that you never forget that these decisions directly affect people's lives.

If this is not too quixotic a statement, then perhaps it is everybody's duty to try to leave the world, in some small way, a better place. Improved profit margins may do this in one way, but if they are at the cost of unnecessary human suffering, then they have not been worth while. So look for ways of implementing the changes with maximum compassion, tolerance, and recognition of the people element.

Hardiness and humility

To make change happen you must be able not only to make the hard decision but also to be taught enough to accept criticism, face up to failure, and take set-backs or discouragement in your stride. The person who is capable of pushing ahead despite the odds is a valuable asset in any situation but these people, who probably have high controller/taker (CT) scores, may well be prone to arrogance. The successful person can become drunk with success, intolerant of the less successful, and regard others as mere pawns in the game. One of the least pleasant examples of this can be seen in Roger Greenaway's description of Robert Maxwell who in *The Downfall of Robert Maxwell* is frequently portrayed as taking delight in the public humiliation of his subordinates. True leaders are respected, not feared, and respect is *not* given for qualities of arrogance but for being 'human'. Being human involves not putting oneself above others but displaying patience, empathy, and understanding through listening to others, receiving feedback, and not dismissing alternative options out of hand.

Perseverance and perspective

There is an old Scottish saying: 'Dogged does it'. Similar to hardiness is the quality of perseverance. The main difference is that the ability to persevere focuses more on the talent of being able to see it through to the end and achieve results. This is an admirable quality, but once again can have its downside. The 'dogged' individual can become like the rhino who will charge and achieve such speed and momentum that it will not change direction even if the target of its charge moves. So, while doggedness is a quality to be admired, it must be balanced with a sense of perspective. Add a little adaptor/dealer (AD) to your approach. More about the rhino later.

The perspective is achieved by deliberately standing back and asking oneself difficult questions. 'Is the problem still the same one that I set out to solve? Has someone else come up with a better idea? What else could I be doing to get results?' The resultant sense of perspective should mean that you achieve the right focus on the situation to guarantee a flexibility that makes perseverance much more likely to achieve the desired result.

Summary

This chapter has focused not so much on the types of changes that are occurring in the world today as on the demands made by change on individuals, especially those tasked with making change happen—with leading. Indeed, it could well be argued that as many changes that occur are so often unforeseen and unpredictable, any book on the 'what' of change must be overtaken by events—and disproved.

The human element in change scenarios, however, remains the one constant. For example, people are portrayed in early literature as going through the transition curve (think of Robinson Crusoe), and the demands on effective yet balanced leadership have remained constant even if those demands are becoming more acute as the pace of change increases. In the final analysis it is the necessity of *giving meaning* to the situation that is the crucial demand made on the leader.

If, in the final section of the chapter, the emphasis appeared to be more on how to avoid failure than on how to succeed, this was deliberate. It is in the lack of balance and excessive behaviour that the seeds of decline are sewn.

Your WIFMs from this chapter

- What changes have you seen, or even initiated, in your organization? How else could they have been introduced?

- How ready are both you and those working with you to assimilate change?

- What could you do to make yourself more ready?

- Are any of your colleagues suffering from the effects of change? What can you do to help them?

- How do you think you change when under pressure and what messages does this send to others?

- Do you manage to maintain a balanced approach when managing change?

Why leaders fail

Introduction

When Margaret Thatcher was ousted from power in late 1990, the cynics joked that she had passed her 'sell by' date. This implied that, no matter what talents she might once have had as a prime minister and leader, there would come an inevitable time when these talents would fade or be outdated. Is that the case? Is a decline in the ability to lead effectively and with relevance inevitable, or is it something that can be avoided?

Earlier in this book we looked at the process of birth, growth, and maturation of leadership. In retrospect, this process appears to be both inevitable and desirable for the majority of those who take on roles or jobs that require leadership as well as management. I concluded that the most effective way that an individual can be propelled through the initial stages of the process was through the exercise of choice. It is through knowledge of one's self, the development of true self-esteem, and an awareness of the different choices of approach to leading that the qualities of leadership can be discovered and allowed to flourish.

This chapter examines the ingredients of decline in leadership as well as the symptoms. It will look at the subtle ways in which qualities can deteriorate and even fester, it will show how the effectiveness of leadership both influences and is influenced by the company culture in which it is found; it will examine both the internal and external causes of decline; and finally tackle the intricate cocktail of willpower, sensitivity, and luck that is required to beat the decline. Above all, it will argue that the qualities, processes, and decisions required to beat the decline are much the same as those that are required to initiate the growth of leadership qualities in the first place.

A LEADER IN FULL DECLINE

Members of the export division of a subsidiary company of Fisons had the dubious privilege of witnessing their general manager moving swiftly through a downward spiral. What made it worse for them was that the top management of the organization did not appear to recognize what was going on, as the division was still riding on a wave of prosperity resulting from good marketing in the past and a healthy demand for the range of products in the Third World.

The general manager had been in the business for most of his working life. He had been a founder member of the international division and had led it for 15 years. It had been his energy that had built up the division, his dedication and extensive travel overseas that had opened up new markets, and his ability to select both people and product that had made the division the one that everyone had wanted to join. But that was in the past!

Now, aged 61 and with 4 years until his retirement, everything had changed. He had suffered a heart attack the previous year and, although this had not affected his health in a major way, it caused a noticeable change in his behaviour and, more important, in the subsequent morale of the division. The main symptom of the new behaviour was a form of paranoia that exhibited itself in a number of alarming and demotivating ways. The energy was still there, in fact it seemed to be greater than ever, however it was now channelled into behaviour that had a very negative effect on all around him and eventually on the profitability of the business.

The energy that had once been channelled towards growth now appeared to be driven by fear. Whereas he had previously enjoyed a reputation as an effective delegator and developer of people, this now changed dramatically. The general manager now spent more and more of his time meddling in the work of his subordinates. He openly voiced his distrust of their decisions and was known to inspect people's desks while they were at lunch in order to check what they were doing. Responsible managers were driven to fury to find notes questioning their decisions and sometimes even correcting their grammar on their return.

Coupled with this practice, the general manager started to criticize his subordinates in front of their peers, yet at the same time openly had favourites. The main problem was that the favourites happened to be the less talented people in the division—those least likely to represent a threat.

An atmosphere of fear and secrecy prevailed, made worse by the fact that the general manager openly boasted about his past achievements but made fewer and fewer efforts to repeat them. Suggestions for innovation and new initiatives were stamped on until the inevitable happened, talented people began to leave.

For a while the general manager was able to explain this exodus to market forces and the fact that he 'developed people so well'. However, when this combination of factors meant that the division unnecessarily lost one of its best customers, an acknowledged cash cow, the organization finally realized that something was sadly wrong and moved the general manager sideways.

Unfortunately, even then he interfered with his successor to such an extent that the organization had no alternative other than to retire him early. Four years of potentially valuable contribution had been lost.

The ingredients of decline

The above example demonstrates a number of the symptoms of a rapid decline in leadership ability. The symptoms are what was observed—and felt—by those on the receiving end. However, what lies behind the symptoms? What causes the decline to happen?

The ingredients or causes may be varied and complex. After all, decline may be exhibited in a variety of ways ranging from an extreme fear of success in others (as illustrated by Lee Iacocca's description of Henry Ford Jr who, he states, dismissed him because his progress represented a threat) to the inertia of the leader who simply runs out of energy, interest, and enthusiasm. It is the cause, however, that must be examined. Most of us at some time or other in our working lives have lived with the effect and by then the damage is usually being done, either to the organization or to ourselves. The key lesson to be learnt is that of how we can recognize the danger signals of our own potential decline and thereby avoid inflicting the damage on others.

The key ingredients are:

- The pressures of power
- An inability to continue learning
- Loss of touch with reality
- The misuse and overuse of strengths
- Insensitivity to company culture and people's expectations
- Fair wear and tear

The pressures of power

The old saying that 'Power tends to corrupt and absolute power corrupts absolutely' is well known. It conjures up pictures of leaders indulging in orgies of Caligulan decadence, of tyrants controlling the lives (or deaths) of thousands with a wave of the hand. It is, however, hardly an image that is applicable within the respectable offices of modern-day business and commerce. Or is it?

The frightening thing about existing in even late 20th century work environments is the amount of power that individuals can exert over one another. Legislation may exist to curb the more Draconian acts of whim, but the fact remains that people whose faces no longer fit still can be ousted from organizations. Bosses can cripple their subordinates' careers through indifferent appraisals or drive them to paroxysms of frustration by ignoring their ideas and suggestions. As the vast majority of those at work are totally dependent on their success there for both their material and emotional well-being, it is not stretching the argument too far to say that those who have control over their success, or at any rate the value that is placed on their efforts, have enormous power over their subordinates. The power may not be a Caligulan power of life or death, but all bosses know that they can drastically affect, by the way they use their power, the sense of security, of self-esteem or of ability to care for dependants, of those that work for them. This is an awesome power. It is an even greater responsibility.

Power exists at all levels in an organization and not just at the very top. Although some may have the decision-making responsibility to close whole units and make scores of people redundant, others at supervisory level still have surprising amounts of power to affect the working lives, and consequently the overall well-being, of those who report to them. The pressures of power, with their accompanying seductive pitfalls, lie in wait for all those who have it—at any level.

Detachment and superiority

This is one of the most obvious yet most alluring traps. Often those who achieve promotion become isolated from former peers. Indeed, they are frequently discouraged from continuing too close associations. After all, how can you make objective or tough decisions about others if you are still 'one of the boys, or girls'. This is logical and to some extent desirable, so long as new leaders do not lose a sense of perspective about their relative importance.

It is when the initial detachment of association leads to detachment of feeling about other people that the problems arise. This can lead to callousness or, worse, a feeling of superiority over subordinates. 'We are all here to get a job done' descends into: 'They are there to serve me.' From there, it is but a small step to start telling yourself that you are in charge because you are more talented, more creative, more forceful, or even a superior form of being, to the others. The rot has set in.

I recall the extraordinary effects on Plessey executives of being given company cars upon reaching a certain grade. The cars were more expensive and prestigious than the average company car and clearly indicated that the executive had 'arrived'. The car owners would sweep past lesser mortals as they entered the factory premises, nonchalantly driving their limousines with one hand on the wheel, reality filtered out by tinted windscreens and blazing stereos, emphasizing distance as well as a certain arrogance.

Filtering

As the leader can be expected to be displeased at receiving bad news (after all, in some regimes the bearer of the bad news used to be put to death), it is not surprising that people tend to edit or filter the information that is passed on to the leader. This filtering can mean that the leader constantly lives with a false sense of reality—or in a fool's paradise!

In turn this will mean that the leader can build up a false sense of his or her contribution: 'Things are going well, I must be doing a great job.' This in itself can be dangerous but, if combined with the fact that some subordinates will go out of their way to flatter their boss, either to protect themselves, or as a short-cut to self-advancement, the effects can be catastrophic. Reality is filtered, self-esteem is artificially bolstered, and detachment is enhanced. However, when reality finally catches up, the nonplussed leader may still retain the detachment and strike out with callous cruelty. The filtering has led to an unrealistic conception by the leader of his or her power and worth.

Isolation

This may be aided by filtering of information or may be simply the result of the way that the job is perceived within the organization. The leader may feel insufficiently secure to ask the opinion of others or to reveal secret worries to them. This feeling of isolation, of there being no one to turn to, is one of the most obvious pitfalls of power; it is also one of the hardest to withstand. It can mean that the leader can be driven to behave in excessive ways, either by overusing strengths (as will be explored later) or by making rash, poor, or uninformed decisions.

As shown in countless books, plays and films (to say nothing of real life), the isolation of leadership is one of the hardest pressures to bear. It can lead to poor decisions and, worse, it can lead to paranoia. The leader feels alone, cut off and fears conspiracy. Power once again has got out of perspective and if the effects this time are different, they are no less harmful.

Ego out of control

Perhaps the greatest danger of power is the effect that it can have on your ego. Although it is essential to have self-esteem in order to be an effective leader who does not try to act out insecurities or neuroses through leadership, it is equally important for the leader to retain a sense of humility.

Of course, it is easy to associate the job that you perform with your overall identity as a human being, and if this job appears to place you above others then the sense of identity, of self-importance, becomes inflated. Sometimes the sense of superiority becomes illustrated in various symbols: the distinctive style of dress, the especially decorated office, the catch phrase, and so on. While no leader wants to be thought of as characterless or grey, the leader who invests too much time and energy in the pursuit of image will inevitably start putting out the wrong messages. Good leadership is found in what people do and if they start to place image and desire for admiration above results, if they start to demand respect rather than earn it, then the trappings of power have started to detract from the jobholder's ability to wield it positively.

An inability to continue learning

In order to lead it has been necessary to do a great deal of learning. This will have involved learning about the organization, learning about the markets or environment in which it operates, learning about other people and, of course, learning about one's self. *The learning must continue.* It is when the leader no longer recognizes the absolute need to continue learning that those insidious traps of complacency, laziness, closed-mindedness, and inability to accept or instigate change yawn open.

As the rate of change increases, it is vital that both individuals and organizations adjust and keep up. Those who do not will not survive. Therefore perhaps we should stop referring to leaders as leaders and start referring to them as the 'chief learners'. This in itself would be a refreshing way to look at both the individual leader and the functions of leadership. The process of learning implies both an openness and a sense of humility. If you consider yourself to be a chief learner first and a leader second then you are far less likely to succumb to many of the pitfalls of power and ego intoxication already described. But how can this approach to leading be learnt? There are a number of essential messages.

Keep questioning

When you stop asking questions you stop learning. It is vital to maintain a keen inquisitiveness about people, events, trends, causes, and effects. The opposites of inquisitiveness are boredom and complacency and they are quickly transmitted to others. However, inquisitiveness, as demonstrated by an eager questioning technique, will not only keep you learning but also sharpen the respect of those around you.

Look for new approaches

One of the strongest brakes on personal creativity is the trap of thinking that there is only one way of doing things. It is vital to look for new approaches and, if you cannot think of any yourself, to question others and to accept their suggestions where practical. In doing this it will be necessary to look on others, and perhaps especially subordinates, as people from whom you can learn. The leader must therefore become a coordinator of the organization's or department's learning, in other words, lead the learning from the middle. This is not easy, it means putting aside many of the popular preconceptions of what leaders should do or be, but it is a key element in beating the decline.

Avoid the learning disabilities

It is easy to state that leaders should seek to continue to learn, but all too easy to ignore the traps that make learning itself difficult. In *Leadership in the Fifth Dimension*, Peter Senge identified what he called the 'seven learning disabilities'. While these disabilities were set in a wider organizational systems' context than is dealt with here, four of them are well worth examining as they aptly illustrate how people can convince themselves that they are learning when in fact they are not. They also show how a misconception of their position can totally cloud their judgement.

1. *I am my position*   Over time, people in organizations begin to identify closely with their positions, in other words, *who they are* and *what their purpose is*. This can lead to a myopic view of the organization where it is impossible to see the consequence of one's actions on the organization and its systems.

2. *The enemy is out there*   This is a by-product of the 'I am my position' mentality. A result of over-identification with the job is the fact that if things go wrong it is all too easy to imagine that somebody else 'out there' was at fault. If the enemy out there is always at fault then it is difficult to be objective and to see the real solution.

3. *The illusion of taking charge*   True learning should lead to proactivity, but too often proactiveness can mean that the individual decides to be more active in fighting the enemy out there. Senge states that if we believe that the enemy is out there and we are 'in here' then proactiveness is really reactiveness in overdrive. True proactiveness comes from seeing how our own actions contribute to our problems.

4. *The delusion of learning from experience*   Senge says that we learn best from experience but that we never experience the results of our most important decisions. The most important decisions made in organizations have systemwide consequences that stretch out over years or decades. While I do not agree with this theory as a sweeping generalization (usually the results of our decisions catch up with us all too soon), it is true to say that consequences may be delayed and that consequently it is necessary to avoid the trap of drawing the wrong conclusions from the consequences (or non-consequences) of one's actions.

It is interesting to note that preoccupation with self is the root cause of most of the learning disabilities, just as it is such an active component in the more destructive pressures of power.

Look to learn from everything

While it is common advice that you should learn from everything you do, it is less common advice to insist that one should especially seek to learn from one's difficulties. This is, in fact, blatant common sense and it might seem logical to think that learning from difficulty was common practice. However, the results of a wide-ranging survey (unpublished) carried out by Sundridge Park through interviews with a large number of managers indicated that most had not taken the opportunity to reflect on what they might have learnt from their difficulties, regardless of whether or not they were of their own making. What a loss of opportunity!

An old saying goes: 'Never be ashamed to admit that you were wrong, it is the same as saying that you are wiser now than you were yesterday.' How true! Unfortunately most managers had not given their mistakes or misfortunes enough thought truly to admit that they were now wiser, that in fact they had gone on learning. The advice for individuals incorporated in the report is well worth repeating here as general advice for leaders who need to 'beat the decline':

1. Undertake your own review of difficulties you have encountered in your managerial life and what you have learnt from them.

2. Consider the opportunities available to you for sharing your problems or difficulties with other people, and associated opportunities for learning from that sharing.

3. Consider opportunities for discussing learning opportunities not necessarily in relation to a specific difficulty with one or more colleagues or individuals outside the organization.

4. Set out, as a result of these actions, the benefits you might accrue from undertaking them. Then set out the benefits that might be derived for you as a learner.

Loss of touch with reality

When I worked for Ernst and Whinney, the firm's insolvency function had devised a semi-humorous list of features that partners said might indicate that an organization was about to go bust even before they had looked at any of the figures. These features included:

- Company recently achieved Queen's Award for Export
- Rolls-Royce in car park
- Flag-pole outside head office
- Fish tank in reception
- CEO recently elected as president of local chamber of commerce.

Despite being a cynic's definition, these features were observable in a surprising number of insolvency cases. As is the case with much cynicism or humour, it was effective because it contained a large element of truth. But what did the existence of these features really signify?

On the surface they meant that there was a probable loss of contact with the basic business realities, that the people running the business were no longer concentrating on those essentials upon which the business was founded. There is, however, a more sinister angle. Why had executives lost touch? How was it that a preoccupation with self had replaced concentration on business essentials? What effect might this have on the organization?

PRICE LEAD OR BUST

A medium-sized advertising agency was in an interesting position. It had a good name in the in the advertising world and was known as a reliable provider of bulk rather than prestige advertising. Its reputation for solid, reliable service had been built up by the outgoing chief executive who was known and respected in the advertising world. His successor was promoted from the board. Powerful, tough, and persuasive, she wanted to change the organization's image to push it into a more prominent and prestigious position.

The mechanism for this was to be price. If the top agencies had higher fee rates then so would this organization and, over a short period, prices were pushed up rapidly. There were strong reactions from both within and without the agency.

Clients complained and compared the 'price hikes' unfavourably to the rate of inflation. Account executives passed back their comments but were either ignored or penalized for taking a critical approach. Soon it became safer to go along with the strategy than to stand against it and the price rises continued. Larger, more up-market offices were then acquired before the full effect of the pricing strategy was known.

Unfortunately, the CEO and her board ignored two vital issues in their race for prestige via price leadership. The first was that price increases can be supported only by an increase in the value of the offering (and after the creative director had resigned this became less likely), while the second was that the recession meant that there was an overall fall in the level of expenditure on advertising by the agency's existing and prospective clients.

This loss of a sense of reality, an adoption of a highly controller/taker approach, had initiated this particular leader's decline almost before she had properly started.

The immediate result was a massive fall in revenue coupled to increased fixed costs. Both the CEO and her board ignored the overt warning signs, adopting the philosophy that major changes took time and that they must have the courage of their convictions. Unfortunately, many of their oldest clients did not share this conviction. Neither did the receiver!

What was evident here was a case of the leader's obsession causing those closest to her to lose touch with the realities of the business, a case of destructive influence upon the business. It was a case of what Manfred Kets de Vries describes as a 'Folie à Deux'—sharing the madness around.

Put bluntly, a *folie à deux* is a case of a leader's driving his or her followers mad. What this really means is that the strong, and often unopposed influence of the leader breeds a contagious instability of behaviour and culture within the organization. Kets de Vries in *Prisoners of Leadership* cites a number of prime causes for this strange, but not uncommon, phenomenon. They are:

- A strong leader with a compelling message
- Followers who are insecure or who feel a strong need for firm direction
- Low level of outside influence
- A situation where compliance is seen as easier than confrontation (and perhaps safer!)

Many of these features can be seen to exist where a political dictator has gained power, but they can exist with equal ease in an organizational context. After all, if your livelihood is dependent upon your relationships within the organization then opposition takes courage. In entrepreneurial organizations based on a single powerful individual, *folies à deux* are even more likely to exist. The results are predictable, unproductive behaviour reigns supreme, and the firm can lose contact with its original goals and objectives.

Recognizing the symptoms

One of the most frightening facts about *folies à deux* are that the prime perpetrators do not realize what is happening and that those who do are powerless to change the situation. It is important, however, to examine some of the main symptoms, if only as a warning to potential perpetrators, or victims. Briefly they can be summarized as follows:

1. *Toe the party line 'or else'*   There are politically correct ways of thinking or doing. Follow them and you will survive and prosper—ignore them and you are, to put it mildly, suspect. The terrible thing about political correctness, in whatever context it is found, is that it stifles self-expression and ultimately the truth.

2. *Lack of creativity*   A by-product of toeing the line. If there is but one acceptable approach how can originality and creativity survive except in some disfigured form?

3. *High level of secrecy*   The in-crowd control information and release it on a 'need to know' basis. Information control is clearly power and the next step to information control, of course, is information collection—on other members of the organization. If this sounds too much like 1984 to relate to business life then think again, many existing organizations reflect varying degrees of this symptom, perhaps even your own!

4. *People problems*   The independent-minded find it hard to exist in *folies à deux* while sycophants love them. Consequently, there may be a high turnover of executives or, alternatively, peculiarities in succession and promotion as the 'yes people' move upwards.

5. *Eccentricities of strategy and planning*   As was seen with the advertising agency, strategies can be pursued in 'bull at a gate' fashion at the expense of reality and good sense. Under leadership that has lost touch with reality, strategies may reflect the overriding preoccupation of the leader and drive the organization lemming-like towards oblivion. The effects will be examined more closely later in this chapter.

Curing the *folie à deux*

The easiest way to cure it is to separate the people. This of course is easier said than done, especially if you are a victim rather than someone with any control over events. If, however, you are in a position of control and see this situation in any part of the organization then action is called for. Outsiders such as auditors, customers, suppliers, consultants, and contractors can be involved to reflect a different form of reality. It is when people refuse to listen to any outside opinion that they are at their most dangerous.

A situation of *folies à deux*, or indeed any situation where power has got out of control, is the antithesis of an empowerment culture. If one of the best things that good leader can do is to grow other leaders, then a culture that, through fear of reality, insists that all followers simply toe the party line just results in what can be called the *Russian doll syndrome*. The analogy is simple but powerful. If you open up a Russian doll you will find an exact replica of the original contained therein. The trouble is, it is a smaller, less significant version and if the process is repeated the replicas become smaller and smaller. Any true leadership culture should aim to produce larger and larger dolls, for the good of all.

The *folie à deux* is one situation where whole groups of people can lose touch with reality. The initial contagion, however, usually stems from one individual. Where does the initial loss of contact then initiate, and what can be done about it?

Reality-testing yourself

Many of the causes of the loss of contact with reality have already been examined. The particular pressures of detachment from others, filtering, and isolation can have a strange effect on one's sense of perspective, and the higher you climb, the less chance there is of criticism or challenge. The antidote lies in a level of critical self-examination. Some of the more searching questions that you can ask yourself could be on the following lines:

- When did I last really listen to my subordinates?
- Do I value them for their real worth or simply because they appear to support me?
- Do I ever stop to examine my vision? Is it still relevant? Does it stand up to questioning?
- Am I seeing things only in terms of black or white? Or do I acknowledge that shades of grey may exist and better reflect reality?

It may not be easy to answer all of these questions perfectly truthfully for one's self. After all, it may be easier to maintain the self-deception. One demanding way to ensure that the questions are answered truthfully and indeed to obtain candid feedback on other aspects of your leadership style is to find a mentor. The mentor could be someone in a similar position, the previous jobholder, or someone still within your area who is, for example, approaching retirement and who has no fear of retribution if harsh feedback is called for. Whoever the mentor is, that person should understand your role but have a high degree of independence from you— the benefits will be considerable, even if the process is occasionally painful.

The misuse and overuse of strengths

Thomas Carlyle once stated a simple but compelling truth: 'The ideal is in us but the impediment is in us also.' In other words, an overused strength can easily become a weakness. Over reliance on a set of behaviours will bring about the increasing certainty of their inappropriate use and what people once used to praise you for can quickly become the object of their criticism. Napoleon Bonaparte summed it up. 'From the sublime to the ridiculous is but one step.'

In Chapter 8, we examined the LIFO® model of human behaviour as a means of illustrating how people may react to the pressures of change. For each positive behaviour there was a negative counterpart. The resourceful controller could become the destructive taker, the meticulous conserver could become the clinging, nit-picking holder and so on. When under pressure people could emphasize a behaviour to excess or significantly change their predominant type of behaviour thereby causing themselves to appear unpredictable or bizarre.

A leader in decline can easily over emphasize a behaviour trait or, through the pressures of leadership, go into excess in one or other of the LIFO model styles. By doing this the leader may not exhibit enough of some of the more positive characteristics and then behaviour will be out of balance. There is, in fact a vicious circle, a leader may 'go into excess' because of fear of failure and thereby accelerate the decline On the other hand, the overuse of a strength, simply because it has achieved results in the past, may in turn start the process of decline. The new CEO of the advertising agency went into an excess of controller/taker behaviour, infected others with those values and consequently engineered her own downfall as well as that of the organization. A healthy dose of conserver/holder behaviour to temper the high controller/taker orientation would have led to a more balanced and productive approach to planning.

As seen, the effects of excessive behaviour and the unproductive use of power on an organization and its strategies can be alarming. Manfred Kets de Vries has produced interesting work on what he called the 'Characteristics of Neurotic Organisations'. He states that the neuroses stem from the mind set of the leader and create problems in culture, organization and strategy. I have adapted this approach to fit a 'LIFO in excess model' and concentrated on more general effects upon the organization as a whole.

1. *Excess of controller/taker behaviour*   The leader's behaviour becomes arrogant, domineering, controlling in all respects. The approach becomes over-focused and obsessive with the result that subordinates become slavish, insecure and therefore less creative. Dependent upon the whim of the leader, strategies can become either mercurial, obsessive and inconsistent or unadaptive and slow-moving as people cover their backs as the first priority.

2. *Excess of supporting/giving-in behaviour*   Everybody likes the leader who relates well to others but when the supporting turns to giving-in, when the tough decision is avoided because people are involved, when concern becomes perceived as weakness it is probable that the organization will lose a sense of direction. Mediocrity may be tolerated and then becomes the norm. Standards will slip and initiative will become a thing of the past. The organization will eventually lose the ability to rise to new challenges.

3. *Excess of conserving/holding behaviour*   When conserving becomes holding, the concern for method and detail can get out of control. Decisions are put off while facts and figures are exhaustively analysed. Change is seen as a threat and analysis of information and trends used as a means of delaying decision making. This will result in frustrated subordinates and a clinging to established procedures, mature markets and existing products. In times of change this approach will inevitably lead to a crisis although the awareness of its arrival may be long delayed.

4. *Excess of adapting/dealing away behaviour*   The person who favours adaptive behaviour, so good at getting things started, so good with people, so able to find new approaches to problem solving will, in excess, become the dealer away. The behaviour, usually so productive changes to that of vacillating, indecisive, inconsistent, appeasing and perhaps even frivolous. Sometimes the leader as a result of the vacillating, may appear detached. Certainly those looking for strong direction and clear leadership will be disappointed and unauthorized actions or the liberal interpretation of deliberately ambiguous instructions may take place out of sheer frustration. Was the disastrous Charge of the Light Brigade for example, the consequence of excessive 'dealing away' at the top combined with excessive 'taking' at brigade level?

Avoiding the traps

The key message for us all is that most people have it in them to indulge in excessive behaviour of one sort or another. The triggers may lie in the fear that one is 'slipping' as a leader, in discovering opposition to one's ideas, perceiving challenge from a strong rival, the loss of one's vision or even over-preoccupation with the vision. On the other hand, sheer boredom, a feeling of 'here we go, yet again, ' may put considerable pressure on those with a low tolerance of routine. The key is to realize how one might go into excess, to look for signs in others as a method of coaching one's self and to readily accept feedback from others.

Insensitivity to company culture and people's expectations

Company culture is best described as 'the way that we do things around here'. All organizations are different in this respect; when you start to get to know an organization definite differences in approach and in atmospheres soon become apparent. Sometimes these differences are noticeable as soon as you get past reception, sometimes they are more subtle and take longer to appreciate. The culture of the organization will be a product of its history, its product, or service, but most of all of its people—especially the norms and values set by its leaders.

Values

Behaviour is driven by a mixture of pressures, it is also driven by the values held by the individual. Just as individuals should have values, so should organizations. Organizational values will reflect the values of its leadership and these in turn will set the company culture. Often the values are explicit and are set as part of the overall mission statement. A typical set of values for an established, mature organization might include the following principles:

1. *Growth and progress*   All organizations should be looking for opportunities to grow, to innovate, and to seek out new markets. To fail to do so is to court disaster.

2. *Ethical methods and high standards*   It is important that an organization remembers that real progress can be obtained only by the strictest adherence to principles of honesty and quality. The Lockheed scandal and Bhopal disaster show how easily these values can be forgotten.

3. *People and their growth*   These values deal with a range of
   issues centring around how the organization cares for its people,
   develops them, and communicates with them.

It is usually up to the leader to set the culture, based on clearly
understood values. The most fruitful culture is one that generates the
maximum progress while giving as much opportunity as possible for the
people involved to develop and grow. Unfortunately, by no means all
company cultures reflect this, and regrettably it is easy for a company's
culture and values to 'regress' to something less developmental or democratic as the leadership comes under pressure or starts to decline.
    Clues to declining leadership ability may be observed in some of the
following impacts on a previously mature organization's values and
culture:

- Reorganizations proliferate, but achieve little. Often they just
  reinforce status gaps.

- Suggestions and new ideas are no longer welcomed.

- Different and often conflicting messages from 'the management'
  abound, with the result that people take fewer initiatives and
  organizational politics abound.

- There is a preoccupation with measurement and checking which
  drives staff into child-like rather than mature responses.

- The original vision dies and is no longer reflected in policy.

- Often the message from above starts with a list of rules dictating
  how both procedures and those responsible for operating them will
  be improved.

As can be seen, many of these 'clues' are preoccupied with the *how* and
the *what*, with rules and processes (even if unclearly stated), rather than
with allowing staff freedom of action, expression, or teamwork. They are
part of what Roger Harrison calls a *transactional culture*, a form of
culture that many organizations start with and progress upwards from,
but then all too often revert to if their leader or leaders start to decline.

The three levels of organizational culture

Roger Harrison has produced much of the most valuable work on organizational culture and its development over the years. His latest work divides the
cultures to be found into three main types—*transactional, self-expression,*
and *mutuality*—and he states that they exist as a kind of hierarchy through

which organizations must evolve. The problem is that organizations can sink back to their previous state if their leadership allows this to happen.

Transactional cultures

These are usually highly hierarchical and operate through a high degree of control of individuals. An atmosphere of reward and punishment and stick and carrot exists. Rules exist and proliferate while individuals compete with each other for power, status, and reward.

The strategies of the organization will be orientated towards quick gain and profit and may well react to events rather than take on new initiatives. This has been the pattern for most organizations over the centuries and Harrison argues that the modern organizations that are going to succeed must grow out of it.

Self-expression cultures

These are much more autonomous and egalitarian. They operate through the individual's ability to help it achieve or make an impact in the marketplace. As such, individuals in these cultures will be rewarded on their individual (or individualistic) contributions to the organization's success, and internal competition will centre around observable individual excellence and problem-solving. This will fit in with the firm's strategies in the marketplace which are liable to be experimental and risk-taking. Rewards will be high for the successful, but the atmosphere will be that of sink or swim.

Many people recognize that they are working in self-expression cultures and, because this fits their own needs and ambitions, are very happy to be doing so.

Mutuality cultures

This is the most mature form of culture and organizations can evolve through the other forms into it. It is best characterized by feelings of mutual cooperation and contribution. The firm itself will be orientated towards quality of response and service. To achieve this it recognizes that there must be high levels of communication and trust within it. Its systems must serve its people as well as the task—not the other way round. People within the firm will be motivated to produce excellence in cooperation with each other. Teamwork and mutual support will flourish to the benefit of staff, the organization, and its customers.

This is not an easy culture to achieve and it depends on the quality of the organization's leadership to make it happen. Interestingly, studies have shown that most individuals consider that they work in cultures with too much transaction and not enough mutuality. It seems to be a state that most wish for but few truly experience.

The challenge to the leader

As a mutuality culture is essentially one with high levels of individual empowerment combined with the encouragement of teamwork, it is one that leaders should strive towards. Of course, the quality and maturity of the staff involved are a factor here but, once again, this is another challenge to the leader. Leaders in decline, or who fear decline, are likely to spread an atmosphere of fear or of confusion through indulging in high controlling/taking, conserving/holding or adapting/dealing away behaviour. None of these atmospheres is conducive to cooperation, mutuality, or the joint learning that mutuality implies.

If one of the causes of decline is the inability to continue learning, then possibly one of the greatest challenges to a leader will be that of continuing personal growth through the encouragement of learning, teamwork, and mutual support within the organization. This is easier said than done and will require reappraisal of the leader's own values and approaches. The results, however, will be invaluable and will result in what has come to be known as the 'learning organization', first mentioned in Chapter 7.

The 'learning organization' as an expression is not very helpful. What it in fact refers to is an organization where working and learning are virtually the same thing. Great emphasis is put on continuous improvement so that through the way it does its business, the organization is always increasing its ability to solve problems and exploit new opportunities. Processes, systems, and structures combine to create a climate in which people's learning is valued as the organization's main competitive advantage. All levels of staff are involved through thoughts on quality, methods, and approaches to work and so the organization can continually adapt to its environment and stay ahead. It is continually adding to the value of its offering and contribution through the way that it stimulates and encourages its people.

To achieve these lofty heights, the leader must provide opportunities for people to learn and must encourage them to do so. People must also be encouraged to share their expertise with each other rather than hanging on to it as individuals would do in a self-expression culture.

The challenge to the leader is complex, but achievable. It involves work and careful analysis both of self and, through the organization, of others. Sensitivity is required along with a mature attitude towards power. The decline should be avoidable, but this brings us back to where we started. Do we all have a sell-by date and, at best, is it merely postponed?

Fair wear and tear

So is decline inevitable? Insofar as old age and death are inevitable, it must be. However, insofar as we are not talking about leading to the bitter end, as in the case of Franco or Tito, but about leading within an organizational context where for most there is a set retirement date, my thesis is that it can be avoided.

Of course, as the years pass the body ages and the ability to learn slows down. However, the cult of youth would have us believe that for the majority of our allotted years we are 'over the hill'. What rubbish! The challenge to everybody, whether they are acting in a leadership capacity or not, is to retain the enthusiasm of their youth and to pace themselves so that the energy is there when it is needed. In many cultures (if not the British culture), the old are accorded especial respect, because with age comes wisdom—and wisdom has been a major prop for leaders from Solomon onwards.

So, the decline is something that many people allow to happen—it is not an inevitable event within the working life of most leaders. There is a difference between out-growing one's role and declining as a leader. For most, a particular leadership role is part of a career and the time may come to move on to bigger things. If the new role contains a major element of leadership then the essentials already learnt will still apply even if they are to be put to work in a new context.

Above all, it is necessary to realize that the decline in leadership ability can happen and that for those who allow themselves to go stale, who stop learning, it will. But leadership itself is about change, about creating movement, challenges, and development, therefore by implication, true leaders should not go stale and should be able to weather the wears and tears of time. Managers may decline, it should be harder for leaders. Churchill, Golda Meir, and others embarked on major leadership roles at an age, and after pasts which should have made them ready to accept retirement willingly. In fact, they went on to accept challenges that would have daunted anybody.

The ability to retain interest and enthusiasm and to continue to learn and embrace the future are key factors. If I may be permitted an indulgent personal recollection. My Grandmother led the Tunbridge Wells branch of the WRVS (Women's Royal Voluntary Service) for over 40 years: staleness and the concept of not embracing the new, never crossed her mind. Eventually, in her early eighties, she decided to retire. A holiday was called for and as it was to be in Italy, she taught herself fluent Italian.

The leadership health check

1. Are you still interested in your job and in its 'people' elements?

2. What sort of culture do you feel most happy creating around you? Have you stopped to think what other people might appreciate?

3. How happy are you about ambiguous situations? Are they a challenge or a headache?

4. How often do you stop to assess your behaviour or your reactions to people? Have you ever considered that you may be 'going over the top'?

5. Do you still have a clear vision of what you want to achieve and do you state it with conviction? Or is it now just expressed in trite slogans?

6. How do you feel about suggestions and ideas from others? Are they essential or a nuisance?

7. Badges of office are an essential prop for the senior person and information is a powerful tool that must be husbanded with care. True or false?

8. Is adapting, learning, and encouraging others to learn exciting and necessary, or just a bore?

Summary

If willpower and sensitivity and the ability to continue learning are major factors then luck has not been mentioned, but that is a capricious factor well outside the scope of this chapter. Or is it? There is the true story of the professional golfer who holed out from a difficult position in a bunker. 'That was a lucky shot,' shouted a spectator. The golfer turned to him, 'One per cent luck and ninety-nine per cent damned hard work!' he replied.

Over and above this element of hard work, a willingness to learn and to acknowledge the pressures of power are required. An ability to work within an agreed framework of what is considered to be right and just is also essential. Leaders have a responsibility to uphold standards, be they legal, moral, or ethical, and it is not good enough to excuse failure here as simply reflecting the spirit of the times.

Outside the town of Lewes in Sussex stands a monument commemorating the battle that was fought there in 1265. In it, Simon de Montfort defeated Henry III, thereby curtailing the power of the king and laying the basis for the first parliament. On the monument are inscribed the following words: 'Law is like fire, for it lights as truth, warms as charity, burns as zeal. With these virtues as his guide the King will rule well.' Lying within this exhortation are many perennial elements of good leadership.

So it does take hard work and more, both to be and to stay a leader. Other talents are necessary and will become more so in future, as will be seen in an examination of the *millennium leader*.

Your WIFMs from this chapter

- Are any of the pressures of power affecting you?

- Are you still eager to learn ?

- What effect do you have on your subordinates (or your boss on you)? Is it always healthy?

- Have you considered the dangers of overuse of a strength? Can you recognize the symptoms?

- What is the prevailing culture in your workplace? Is it the one you wish to see and can you do anything about it?

- Do you still welcome new ideas?

- How often do you feel the need to check up on the work of others?

Beating the decline
The millennium leader—
creative, strategic, and sure-
footed

Introduction

In Chapter 9, much emphasis was placed on the need to keep learning, to continue growing in order to avoid the slip into decline. The leader may have to change the mode of thinking to that of chief learner, stimulator and propagator of excellence, rather than simply that of the one who gives directions.

One essential question remains, however. What it is exactly that the leader will have to learn and master, in order to remain a good leader today but more important, to become one of the relevant leaders of tomorrow? Some strong hints have already been given, especially in Chapter 9, but it is now necessary to predict more specifically what will be required of leaders at all levels in the years to come. To talk about the *millennium leader* may be to indulge in the art of catch phrases but, insofar as each century has made different demands on mankind— let alone each decade—it is not unreasonable to look ahead to the particular demands that may be made on leaders as a new millennium looms. The seconds tick down towards it and not only at the Pompidou Centre!

Pressures and demands

Tempting though it may be, it is not the intention to try to predict what is going to happen in the next century. Without a crystal ball or Nostradamus at one's side it is impossible to predict the immediate future, far less to predict years or decades ahead. What comes considerably easier is to examine some of the forces at play today that will, in all probability, have a considerable effect on the way that we do business, live, and die in the years to come.

Among the forces that will probably change the way we live in the future (if they are not arguably doing so already) are:

- Environmental problems and pollution

- Massive changes in methods of communication and dissemination of information

- AIDS

- Movements to and from international currencies

- The economic growth of the Far East

- The decline of conventional religious practices and the growth of fundamental religion

- The race to find new sources of energy

- The decline of the nuclear family

- Overpopulation

- Intermingling of cultures

- Changes in business practice, employment, and in the shape of organizations

- Globalization of business practice

The list no doubt could go on for much longer and I am sure that I must have missed a number of forces that will become major influences in the near future. The key question, however, concerns what they will demand of the leader of the future. In many respects the future is already upon us, but not all leaders by any means are changing to meet it. The indications are that leaders must be both steadfast and flexible, creative and adaptive. They will have to think more strategically and be increasingly aware of the different demands that will be made of them.

All these requirements imply movement. Movement forward but with a sure-footed, lightly stepping tread. What you cannot afford to be is either a boiled frog or a rhino! Perhaps an explanation is required.

In *The Age of Unreason*, Charles Handy refers to the parable of the 'boiled frog'. Apparently if you take a frog from its pond and place it into a pan of very hot water it will notice at once that the environment is hostile and take immediate positive action. In other words, it will jump out. On the other hand, if you take the same frog and place it in a pan of cold water which you then slowly bring to the boil, it will not react to the gradual change in its environment until it is too late. By not reacting it has allowed itself to be boiled alive.

No leader can afford to be a boiled frog in reacting to the demands of the future. By the same token it is equally disastrous to be a rhino. This requires less explanation. The unfortunate rhino is well known for its short-sightedness and its propensity to charge. However, once it has started to charge it can only thunder along in a straight line towards its target. By the time it gets there the target may have moved on and in its head down charge it will have been unaware that there was a hunter (threat!) lurking in one bush and an attractive rhino of the opposite sex (opportunity!) just beside another. Only if the target remains static and unchanging over a long period is the rhino likely to succeed.

What the boiled frog and the rhino have in common is that they have chosen the wrong approach to moving forward. Both are inappropriate and potentially disastrous and whether the forward movement is in response to change, the pressures of business, or one of the forces itemized, it must be flexible, sure-footed, thoughtful, open-minded, and creative. More than ever these are going to be the requirements of successful leadership in the future. None of these requirements are new but the emphasis will change and accentuate them. By the same token, all the existing requirements of dealing sensitively with others, of valuing one's self, of encouraging teamwork, and of motivating and coaching others will still apply. However, without a flexible and sure-footed approach to the demands of the future they will become devalued, as the overall direction may well be wrong.

What then in addition needs to be learnt to ensure that the potential pitfalls are avoided and that the movement forward has all the attributes necessary to give it continuous momentum? The millennium leader will need to have developed a number of skills, although as the years unfold it is possible that new skills or approaches, that at present appear unimportant or have not been considered, may come to the fore. However, at present (minus crystal ball) here are the skills and attitudes that I consider will be the vital ones to be learnt for survival in the immediate future:

- The ability to think more creatively than others.
- The flexibility to handle difficult problems, especially to be able to cope with dilemmas.
- The ability to combine a leadership perspective with strategic thinking and a business-like approach.
- Being aware of and being able to react to the different requirements that will be made of them as leaders.

When these requirements have been examined, the concept of the millennium leader will need to be summarized and a number of old and new demands blended in order to illustrate the variety of challenges, both of learning and doing, that are to be faced. The one concept that most clearly links the old and new demands is that of WIST, and this will be revisited as the requirements come under the microscope.

The ability to think creatively

Much has been spoken and written on the subject of creative or lateral thinking. Among the best known proponents is Edward de Bono who has done a great deal to tease people into examining their approaches to problem definition and solution. But what is it?

It would be foolhardy indeed to attempt to give one definition of the subject because, by its very nature, it enters a number of different areas and presents us with a variety of challenges, some of which cannot be met by everybody. One definition of creative thinking might be 'the ability to tackle problems from a number of different and challenging perspectives'. It is, however, more than this. It involves taking an unconventional approach, looking for the hitherto unseen opportunity; it is the ability to see possibilities where others can only see brick walls, of not accepting the obvious, of challenging the definitions or dimensions of a problem, or perhaps simply creating something new and wonderful whether it be in the realms of art or business. Creative thinking is the art of thinking outside the normal mould. One of its clearest links to the normal business scenario is through Rosemary Stewart's structure of demands, constraints, and choices which invites us to identify and then challenge the constraints facing us through the quality of the choices we make.

What it involves

Putting aside for the moment the question as to whether some people are innately more creative than others, the following characteristics are a necessary prerequisite for creativity in a leader.

Imagination

This, of course, is closely linked to the ability to vision, but we all need time to let our imaginations be productive—or should I say, run riot! The ability to imagine, whether this is the process of daydreaming, or that of creating something new, would appear to be innate in all of us. But to what extent is this ability allowed, or catered for, in most organizations and to what extent do most of us allow ourselves the luxury of exercising our imaginations? We probably spend a lot of time telling ourselves that this fantasizing is self-indulgent and trivial.

The fact is that we need to exercise our imaginations. It helps us to let off mental steam and is also physiologically necessary. The worlds of imagination and dream are closely linked and those who are deprived of sleep for long periods suffer more from dream loss than sleep loss! So, if the exercise of the imagination is necessary, then use it productively. Plan time to dream! Linked to imagination is intuition, which we earlier identified as short-circuited logic and a vital element of WIST. Not everybody has the same inclination towards intuition, but insofar as it is the 'inner voice' as defined by Bennis, then it should be listened to whether it shouts at you or merely whispers. For those who prefer a more logical approach there are many ways that intuition can be subsequently tested— test it by all means, but never ignore it. A combination of imagination and intuition can lead to unique insight into a situation.

Humour

Humour is essentially creative but why is it funny? The laugh factor in a joke usually comes from the introduction of the unexpected, but in a way that is still relevant to the story. In fact many people are at their most creative when they are in the sort of conversation (often towards the end of a good dinner party) where quips, puns, and jokes are flying. People build on what others have said, embellish, improve, and make new connections. What has brought this on? The right atmosphere, a release of inhibitions, and a slight sense of competition. Let it not be said that alcohol is an aid to creativity, far from it, but the release of the creative power of humour without the risk of sanction can lead to new thoughts and ideas. So, an important part of creative thinking lies in daring to think what may at first seem to be the absurd and then in expressing it to see whether in fact there is hidden value there.

Courage

Although there may be nothing so powerful as an idea whose time has come, there will always be those who are ready to ridicule it. In fact, many thoughts, ideas, or concepts that today we take for granted were denounced as absurd when they were first expounded. The monitor evaluator will regard it as a duty to criticize and pick holes. Consequently, one of the greatest barriers to creative thinking, or at least to the stating of the ideas, is the fear of appearing foolish and courage is required to conquer that fear. People are no longer burnt at the stake for expressing new ideas (at least not in business), although careers and reputations can be ruined in different, more insidious ways. So, courage, timing, and judgement are required as travelling companions for the idea.

Patience

This virtue is needed in two respects. First, creativity does not always come to order. Ideas and solutions may be just around the corner but the essential spark may not be ready to ignite them. There is no point in giving up if the creative thoughts do not come immediately—give them a chance.

The second area where patience is required is in waiting for the idea to catch on, to be appreciated. Other people may eventually follow but not immediately and the thoughts may need to be restated several times before they are accepted. Do not lose heart; patience and tenacity are prerequisites.

An objective

Some have the gift simply of creating for the sake of it—be it art, music, or literature. However *most* creative thinking is carried out in order to meet an objective, to solve a problem. It is usually the pressing need that not only produces the most creative solutions but is also most likely to precondition the hearts and minds of others to accept them.

THE WOODEN HORSE

One of the clearest and best known examples of a creative solution being driven by (and illustrating) the five prerequisites is that of the ingenious escape by RAF officers from a prisoner of war camp in the Second World War.

The objective was clear and pressing—freedom! The idea? To dig a tunnel close to the wire using a wooden vaulting horse as cover and as a means of transporting the diggers to and from the tunnel, an imaginative adaption of the Trojan theme. However, this time the objective moved from that of smuggling people in, to smuggling them out. It must have taken courage to first express what must have sounded like one of the most far-fetched plans ever conceived, while the actual execution took limitless patience plus great physical courage as the diggers worked virtually under the very noses of the guards. The courage was backed by a dogged tenacity and sense of humour.

In the end the plan succeeded, largely because the actual idea was so creative that the 'opposition' never even suspected what was going on.

Barriers to creativity

The main barriers to creative thinking are conventionalism, self-doubt, and not accepting that creativity can be grown, or at least nurtured. It is well worth examining these barriers more fully as only by destroying them can the full gifts of creativity be exploited.

Conventionalism

There are always the sceptics or traditionalists who will say that 'that solution will never work' or that 'past practices and approaches have served well enough before so why adopt this crazy new idea?' For those who are afraid of looking foolish, these comments are utterly demoralizing. Nevertheless, nothing would ever be achieved if people shrank from criticism, and it is both the leader's right and duty to accept it when it comes but at the same time not to stop trying to innovate, change, and improve because that is the very essence of leadership.

Think of what the detractors' LIFO® styles may be, as a rewording of the proposition may help dismantle the barriers.

Growing creativity

Most people's self-doubt comes from a suspicion that they are not themselves very creative people and that there is therefore no point in trying. One basic question consequently stands. Is creativity something that can be grown? Insofar as most things improve with practice, the answer must be yes.

Everybody does, of course, have to work within the limitations of their innate talents. Few are sufficiently gifted to become great composers, artists, or inventors. But unless we try, we do not know. More to the point, too many people describe themselves as uncreative or having few ideas. The key thing to do is to challenge one's own uncreativity. This can be done in a variety of ways and often involves playing games and solving problems. The fun element is kept very strong and the penalties for failure are zero. At Sundridge Park we often devote quite sizeable parts of some programmes to encouraging delegates to be creative. From initial light-hearted starts, sessions then require delegates to evaluate their approach to problems and to consider the way in which their thought processes may be curtailed by convention and by not questioning assumptions. Usually, once they have realized that it is all right to state the zany answer, and that it is indeed desirable to step outside the boundaries of their normal thinking patterns, the quality of problem-solving and ideas improves dramatically while the sense of freedom and fun grows. The concept of WIFB (what's in it for the business) is, however, never forgotten.

Someone who has done a great deal to show that we are all possibly more creative than we think is Ned Hermann who, with his theory of *brain dominance*, has illustrated that different people will prefer to use different parts of their brains as a normal part of their thinking process. In other words, the person who is very good at logical calculations will prefer to use the left side of their brain, while the person who is extremely good at self-expression and at developing interpersonal relationships will tend to use the right side.

What Hermann shows us is that there are different types of thinking and that therefore there must be different types of creativity as well as intelligence. Most western educational systems have favoured a very left brain approach thereby giving right-brained children severe complexes about their intelligence and potential contribution. Hermann's emphasis on the different types of intelligence and creativity should therefore liberate many to have confidence in their own particular approaches.

This brings us to another vital challenge for the leader of the future, the challenge of growing creativity in other people. It is unlikely that any leader can lead from the front in all respects (even if that were desirable). Perhaps then another great challenge is that of recognizing and fostering creativity in one's staff, of acknowledging that some will be strong in areas where you are not and of helping those people to develop those strengths as a recognition they have something unique to bring to the party.

Methods of growing creativity

Apart from the mind games mentioned above, a number of more distinctly business-based methods exist. They should be used as often as possible both as a means both of problem-solving and of growing group creativity.

Brainstorming

This should need no introduction other than a plea for its proper and frequent use. I have noticed that the golden rules of leaving prejudices behind, going for initial volume of ideas, suspending judgement, and outlawing criticism until the stream of creativity has dried up does not happen as often as might be expected in business meetings, and that the golden rule of 'seek to make connections between the unobvious' is often ignored. If used for encouraging creativity, brainstorming is a vital aid to innovation and also has the benefit of aiding teamwork. Like all good tools it should be used frequently and correctly.

Mindstorming

Less well known than brainstorming but equally effective, this technique is useful when you are faced with a problem or situation requiring change or innovation which can be solved only by you alone. Sit down with writing material and force yourself to come up with 20 solutions. Some of the ideas will be good and others not. The following day do the same thing and then review the previous day's list. Do similar themes occur? Does what seemed ridiculous yesterday now seen quite practical?

This technique will allow you to suspend your judgement and at the same time will force you to go for volume of ideas. When a number of possibilities are available subject them to a rigorous mental audit. What would be the consequences of doing that? What would be the consequences of *not* doing it? Why do I like that choice? Are the reasons selfish or altruistic? At the end of the process, there ought to be a number of potentially viable options from which to choose.

Using the creative ability

The best thoughts remain merely thoughts until they are applied and so the most important contribution that the leader can make is to ensure that something is done with them. Actions speak louder than words—and certainly louder than thoughts! The best compliment that a leader can pay to either team or individual is to back them on their creative new proposals and to empower them to proceed.

But the way ahead is not always that clear. All too often there are alternative solutions and both leader and staff are impaled upon the horns of a dilemma. This brings us to the second set of vital skills and attitudes necessary for the millennium leader.

Problem and dilemma resolution

As part of their management function, leaders must solve problems. A wealth of problem-solving mechanisms exist, some of them long and complex. Most require an accurate definition of the problem to be made before solutions are sought. However, in the future, problems in the form of dilemmas, brought about by conflicting values or choices, will beset the leader. A dilemma might well be described as a two-dimensional problem, a situation where neither proposed solution is ideal and where there is a host of conflicting values.

Dilemmas are, by their very nature, uncomfortable. They are also on the increase as it becomes harder to look at situations strictly in terms of black or white. There always seems to be a 'Yes . . . but' factor and these tax ethics, values, and intelligence. When confronted with a really difficult dilemma, many turn to authority figures and present *them* with the problem. Consequently, the ability to handle a multiplicity of dilemmas will increasingly become a hallmark of successful leadership. Thomas Carlyle summed it up admirably: 'It is a hallmark of first rate intelligence to be able to hold two conflicting thoughts in mind, and still to be able to function.'

The range of dilemmas that currently face individuals and organizations has been admirably summed up by Rosabeth Moss Kanter in *When Giants Learn to Dance* and by Peter Herriot in *The Career Management Challenge*.

Moss Kanter itemizes a number of contradictory demands that face both organizations and the individuals in them. Some of these dilemmas exist for organizations, for example:

- Get 'lean and mean' through restructuring, while being a great company to work for and offering employee-centred policies such as job security.

■ Communicate a sense of urgency and push for faster execution, faster results, but take more time to deliberately plan for the future.

and some, for the individual:

■ Be entrepreneurial and take risks, but don't cost the business anything by failing.

■ Succeed, succeed, succeed—and raise terrific children.

Herriot claims that there are conflicting pressures, usually based on values, that threaten the overall balance of organizational life and give rise to painful dilemmas. His dilemmas tie in more closely to the ways in which ambiguous organizational policy can handcuff individual initiative:

■ We're valuing change and development but we're also valuing steady loyalty and organizational experience.

■ We're encouraging individual stars but also cross-functional collaboration.

■ We're valuing local initiatives but also nurturing core organisation-wide competencies.

■ We're concerned with individually based rewards and careers, but we value collaborative teamwork.

Herriot states that the answer lies in the fact that an organization should have cultures with certain overarching values that make it possible to hold conflicting values simultaneously in tension with the organization, and that the survivors' culture in the future will be one which actually encourages different values. In principle this is fine, but the responsibility that this will place on leaders at all levels must not be underemphasized.

The fact remains that when dilemmas hit us we become impaled upon their horns in a variety of ways and degrees of severity. They may not be of the wide-ranging, macro nature itemized above, but may be far more individual although nevertheless painful. The onus on the leader then is to understand the nature of the dilemmas and to listen and emphasize so that it becomes possible to articulate that understanding of the situation in order to unlock action in others. This can be done either individually or collectively but it must be done. An important job of leaders will be to solve their own personal dilemmas and then to move swiftly on to enable other people to unlock their own thinking.

Charles Hampden Turner drew up an innovatory plan of how to confront dilemmas creatively which recognizes that a creative tension *can* exist between opposing values. It is a useful process, liberating and challenging. The approach is first outlined below and then elaborated, as it can act as the essential process of dilemma destruction.

How to confront strategic dilemmas creatively

1. *Identify the horns*   Look for the opposing values that characterize the horns (i.e. cost vs quantity, or local control vs central control). It is important to accept that the dilemma exists.

2. *Map your position*   Define the opposing values or difficult choices that form the dilemma as two axes. Then identify where you see yourself. Do you incline more to one than the other and to what extent?

3. *Start processing*   Work to loosen the difference between the two horns of the dilemma. It can help to get rid of nouns that describe the axes and instead add 'ing' to the words. They are now processes that imply movement.

    Senge gives the example of: 'Central control vs local control' now becoming 'Strengthening central office *and* growing local initiatives'.

4. *Put into context*   The advice here is to keep an open mind. For example, do not hold one value as intrinsically superior to another, but look to see whether anything can be done to improve the situations that they both represent.

A CAREER DILEMMA

A purchasing manager went to ask the advice of a colleague over a dilemma. She confessed to being less than happy in her job but wondered whether it was wise to move on as she was terrified of making the wrong move. The advice that worked for her was to devote as much energy as possible not only to improving her existing situation at work but also into looking for another job. It was a difficult juggling act but the positive action involved in coping resulted in the fact that when she did receive another offer it simply crystallized for her the fact that the dilemma had ceased to exist—she now wanted to stay in her present job.

5. *Break the hold of static thinking*   Sometimes a dilemma appears to exist because it is seen only at one point in time. The dilemma may in fact just be one stage in an on-going process. Look ahead. Could it solve itself or might many of the features of the situation change dramatically in the future?

6. *Be aware of cycles*   Sometimes the route to the improvement of

both values in the dilemma may mean that both get worse for a while. Once again, look ahead. What may change in the near future? Do not be discouraged too easily.

7. *Look for synergies*   Can the two opposing values or forces be brought together to achieve something bigger and better than either represents? This is a real challenge and represents the nub of leadership. It may require vision or a change to the vision. It will require creative thinking and in all probability a severe test of your influencing skills. But think of the opportunities. As the old saying goes: 'Life is full of opportunities disguised as insoluble problems.'

Reacting to the different requirements

As the forces that will change the way in which we live gather and manifest themselves, different and new requirements are made of leaders. They will call for open-mindedness but above all a willingness to try new approaches.

I received a salutary introduction to 'future shock' when, as a personnel manager, a fairly senior member of the organization made an appointment with me to discuss 'something personal'. It transpired that this male, 42-year-old quality control engineer had decided to change sex. In addition he was married with a daughter and was determined to remain with his family. The change went ahead and gave both my department and me the challenge of paving the way (in organizational terms) for the day of transition. This meant coping not only with the sometimes violently hostile reactions of this person's colleagues but also with our own personal reactions to what we saw taking place. In the end one of the thorniest problems was that of which lavatory (male or female) the individual should use both before and after the final operation—we had delegations from members of both sexes saying that he/she should not be allowed to use theirs. In the end, the only solution was to designate a toilet for that person's use alone—a privilege shared with the managing director.

So, the requirements may be unforeseen and possibly bizarre. They may occur in a variety of forms but for the present let us deal with the most probable: requirements to do with gender, nationality, and profession.

Gender

Statistics show that not enough women are reaching top management positions. In 1992 the Ashridge Research Group showed that there were only 28 women on the boards of the UK's top 200 companies—a pitiful proportion. When a woman succeeds in a major job, such as Dr Elisabeth

Nelson of Addison Consultancy Group and Taylor Nelson or Kathleen O'Donovan at BTR, it is newsworthy in itself. At Sundridge Park, the proportion of women attending management development programmes reflects the low number of women rising to more senior ranks.

However, the question here is not whether more women should achieve senior leadership positions, but whether there are elements of female thinking and behaviour that will be increasingly called to the fore and whether female characteristics will help provide the answers to tomorrow's problems.

There was a time when men joked that the only successful women they knew were more aggressively masculine in attitude and behaviour than the men they worked with. This may well have been true for some who saw it as the only way to get ahead, but it does not appear to be the way that most women and, in fact, many men wish to lead. So the question remains. What is the difference between men and women and in what way can female characteristics indicate the leadership of the future?

Sandra Bem in *Psychological Androgny* defined a number of characteristics that could be defined as masculine or feminine. She did not mean that only one sex had those characteristics but that some are more likely to be found in one sex.

Male	*Female*
Self-reliant	Yielding
Defends own beliefs	Cheerful
Independent	Shy
Assertive	Flatterable
Strong personality	Loyal
Forceful	Warm
Analytical	Sympathetic
Dominant	Sensitive to others' needs
Willing to take risks	Understanding
Makes decisions easily	Compassionate
Willing to take a stand	Soothes hurt feelings

This is a sample of Bem's characteristics and does not include those that she termed 'neutral'. What Bem believes is that those people who have the flexibility to use both masculine and feminine skills will be the most effective because they will be more able to choose from a wider range of behaviours according to the demands of the situation. Once again, the basic principle of situational leadership arises, but with different ingredients in the recipe

The effective leader will be capable of dominant behaviour when necessary and of a sympathetic approach when appropriate. The ability to move between styles is what Bem calls 'androgyny'. Those who are to be more effective as leaders will have to consider developing a broader range of androgynous skills, irrespective of their sex. However, perhaps the main responsibility for examining the appropriateness of their behaviour will rest with men, as shown by Judy Rosener in her article, 'Ways Women Lead'.

Rosener states that her surveys showed that men and women were likely to adopt different approaches to leadership. Men were more likely to be transactional leaders viewing job performance as a series of transactions with subordinates—rewards being given for good work and punishment for poor performance. Furthermore they were more likely to rely on positional authority to get things done. Women, on the other hand, were less traditional in approach. They were more likely to ascribe their power to hard work, networking, and interpersonal skills.

Rosener described the women's leadership style as 'interactive' because they worked hard to make their interactions with subordinates positive for all involved. Much of this involved attempting to enhance other people's sense of self-worth as they believed that this would energize them. They tried to grow group identity by trying to include subordinates in as many parts of the decision-making process as possible.

Attitudes to power was the other great differentiator. The women in Rosenor's survey said that they would willingly share power and information rather than guard it and that they used this information to validate their decisions, seeing the sharing of power and information as an asset rather than as a liability. They had no wish to hang on to formal authority, having learnt in the past to lead and be influential without it. They saw a main incentive to people being that of giving them a feeling of being valued and an opportunity to learn and grow.

This is all quite a change from traditional command and control systems. It ties in with many of this book's opinions about the duty of leaders to listen, develop others, and continue learning. These skills, moreover, will increasingly be in demand in the future as both the nature of organizations and the nature of the business and social environment change. Let us leave the final conclusions on this subject to Judy Rosener:

> 'As the work force increasingly demands participation and the economic environment increasingly demands rapid change, interactive leadership may emerge as the management style of choice for many organizations. For interactive leadership to take root more broadly, however, organizations must be willing to question the notion that the traditional command and control leadership style that has brought success in earlier decades is the only way to get results. By valuing a diversity of leadership styles, organizations will find the strength and flexibility to survive in a highly competitive, increasingly diverse economic environment.'

In fact, if we stop thinking too much about male or female characteristics but more about *desirable* characteristics of leadership, while at the same recognizing the compelling need for society to enable more women to reach top leadership positions, then both organizations and society will be better equipped to face the future.

Nationality

The world shrinks and races and cultures are forced into closer proximity. Sometimes the results are disastrous but more often when races, nationalities, or cultures are brought together, both sides in time learn to live together while at the same time strongly asserting the cultures and values that are special to them.

As a result, the likelihood of a leader in the world of business leading people of a different race or culture increases. This may happen in the leader's own country due to immigration or, eventually, as a result of the European Union throughout Europe. It is just as likely to take place as a result of doing business overseas or being seconded on an expatriate basis. Whatever the reasons for the contact, a certain number of important facts need to be remembered if you are to avoid the cultural traps that lie in wait.

It is true, of course, that certain facts about leadership seem to hold in all countries and cultures. There is no country that in its history has not had leadership of some sort. Indeed, the need for a leader with a vision appears to be as international a phenomenon as does marriage. It is also necessary for the leader to have credibility—except in the worst cases of tyranny. But what underpins this credibility?

In travelling to many parts of the globe what has struck me is not only the intense similarities between peoples, after all we are all part of the human race, but also the considerable differences. Sometimes the similarities at face value appear to eclipse the differences, but therein lie the dangers, as it is what is unseen, in the form of cultural differences and values, that are often the principal drivers and motivators. Consequently, what may work in one culture may be lethal in another.

A CULTURAL EXOCET

A European-owned organization in Thailand had been managed by a South African CEO for some time. His mission was to improve the management methods and consequently the bottom line. He worked closely with the Thai board and even more closely with his Thai managers. His approach was to change and streamline the business slowly but surely, being ever mindful that his managers were being asked to change ways of operating and thinking that had been instilled over many generations. To be successful, he felt the need to think both as a Thai and as a Westerner.

Eventually, he left the business and the chairman brought in a hard-nosed and energetic European as CEO. This person had a personal mission to turn the business around in a record time. He failed. The only record he set was that by adopting the hardest of Western approaches, he managed in a period of three months, to have lost six of his key Thai managers due to resignation. Of those six, two were suffering from nervous breakdowns! Shortly after this the new CEO was also 'resigned'.

As someone who had helped develop the Thai managers with the first CEO, the tragedy behind the statistics was very apparent to me.

The leader in a foreign country needs to be aware of the differences in approach and the fact that they may not be apparent on the surface. When I have been involved in leadership training in South East Asia, my colleagues and I have always given the Belbin team roles' questionnaire to course members. What is interesting is the fact that few participants slavishly write down every word that 'teacher' utters as we had been led to expect—in fact some course members are a good deal more challenging than British participants. What transpired, however, from the Belbin results was that people in the Far East had far higher scores for team worker, company worker and completer finisher than UK course members, who had higher scores for chairman, plant and shaper.

It is possible that these figures may reflect the reasons for the rise of Eastern economies at the expense of many Western economies. The British have been famous for inventing things and starting businesses but notorious for allowing other nations, who were better at turning ideas into practical realities, to exploit and profit from those inventions. The key to this could lie in cultural approaches to teamwork.

So what should the 'millennium' leader do to avoid the cultural traps? In many respects the requirements are not far different from the norm, but are more intense.

1. *Look, listen and wait*   It takes time to absorb the nuances of another culture and often this learning cannot be rushed. Books about the country can help, but cannot replace experience. For example, on arrival in Argentina in the late fifties, no book had been able to prepare me for the fact that even as a boy, to mention the name of ex-dictator Peron in public could have meant assault or worse.

2. *Give people the courtesy of your full attention*   Rules of polite behaviour vary enormously between cultures but this courtesy seems to be worldwide. It is also a fundamental part of good leadership.

3. *Find out what they expect of you*   Different nationalities have different expectations of leadership based on their history or the level of democracy that they have been used to. Can you deliver their expectation to them while still achieving your own goals? If you can manage this tricky balancing act then you may well have arrived at that desirable scenario—win/win.

4. *Avoid cultural assumptions*   They are seductive and are also the basis of racism. It is all to easy to say that all Italians are excitable, all Jews mean, all Belgians are boring, etc. The fact is that in each case the word *some* is valid and the adjectives are applicable to any nationality in the world.

Once again however, dilemmas raise their ugly head. There *are* national and cultural traits, many of which the nations in question are justly proud. But the mistake is to take such descriptions as totally applicable and to base both assumptions and actions on them. As if to prove it, a humorously cynical description of the socio-religious attributes of the nationalities that make up the British Isles goes as follows: the Scots keep the Sabbath and anything else they can get their hands on; the Welsh pray to the Lord and upon their neighbour; the Irish do not know what they believe in but are willing to fight you for it; while the English believe that they are self-made, thereby relieving the Almighty of that awful responsibility.

The mistake is to take such descriptions as gospel truth and to base both assumptions and action on them.

Profession

Much of what the leader must bear in mind about different nationalities and cultures also applies when looking at the leadership requirements for different professions or types of business. The main difference is that of degree.

Professions and, indeed, whole industries have long histories. Particular types of people are found in different industries and professions, partly as a result of their educational backgrounds and partly as a result of assimilation of culture and history. Once again, stereotypes abound. Solicitors are considered to be meticulous and unemotional and accountants boring, while actuaries are known to be those who found accountancy too exciting. Engineers are thought to be underpaid (that at least is true!) and unimaginative, while marketeers are often seen as hysterical and unrealistic. Once again, there is partial truth in all these stereotypes but the real danger again lies in making blanket assumptions.

In reality, people work for a variety of different reasons. For some the main driver is money, for others it is status, while for many it is the knowledge that they are doing done something worth while. Whatever the predominant reason for working, there will still be a need for the guiding vision and a knowledge that the organization is pursuing a logical and worthwhile strategy. Indeed, it is almost impossible to think of any form of organization that can exist without that.

If you have already had a long immersion in a particular industry or profession the need to be mindful of certain cultural norms will already be obvious to you. However, once again, the main danger lies in the case of the leader who, like the new broom who is brought into a totally new situation and who feels the need to make an immediate impact, goes off at half cock. Often what the new leader perceives to be necessary *is* necessary, but the way in which the changes are introduced almost guarantees opposition. For example, chartered accountants work long hours, but it is a norm of the profession that has been inculcated through the process of studying for demanding professional qualifications while at the same time working long days on audit teams. To ask them for more effort with more frequent assessments will, however, probably get the results you demand. The same cannot be said of much of the teaching profession however (and here I *am* showing my prejudices); the same request to people who work shorter hours and currently with no formal assessments has already brought about howls of protest!

So, what do you need to do when asked to lead in a new environment? The following thoughts may help you reach your goals while avoiding the trip-wires along the way:

1. *Acknowledge the dilemma*   You need to show results but you also need to understand the new situation fully. The pressures of both forces will be felt but remember, unless the situation is understood you may not know whether the results you deliver are of value or whether they will last.

2. *Understand and learn*   The understanding of your new situation can be one of the first major results that you deliver. Without it a true helicopter picture will be impossible. The understanding will deepen over time but without the initial burst of learning the deepening will not follow.

3. *Gather facts and read emotions*   Both of these activities can go together. Many leaders, especially government ministers, have run into difficulties because they have concentrated on the former and neglected the latter. Remember whole professions and whole industries have WIFMs and the results of a collective WIFM that has been ignored can be fearful indeed. So, once again, look, listen, seek the advice of impartial mentors and, above all, only engage mouth after engaging brain.

The results of avoiding the most common trip-wires ought to increase the probability of strategies being successfully accomplished, so it is now necessary to look at the concept of the leader as strategist and business person.

The leader as strategist

In discussing strategy as a concept, it is important to note two things. First, the need to think strategically is important at all levels of an organization above supervisory level and secondly, this section is about definitions of strategy and how to start thinking strategically, rather than about strategic techniques themselves.

One thing is resoundingly clear. No leader can be a true leader without also being a strategist. The problem for many, however, is that the word 'strategy' itself is off-putting. It conjures up images of arcane and complex business practices that are open only to those who have studied business formally and at an advanced level. This need not be the case!

So, what is strategy, and what do you need to do to be both a leader and a strategist? The first step must be to define strategy itself.

Strategy

In many respects strategies and the context in which they operate have already been introduced. It is virtually impossible to define visions and missions without alluding to the strategy that will make them happen. The vision defines the desired future state while the strategy is the grand design of how it will be made to happen.

However, the strategy is far more than a plan. There will be many subplans working within and as part of the strategy. But the strategy remains the grand design that is wedded to the mission and the achievement of the vision. Key differences between plans and strategies are that:

- Strategies require detailed analysis of both internal and external influences.

- Strategies usually operate over a longer time period.

- To think strategically, leaders need to be in possession of certain skills and certain elements of knowledge.

- To be able to think strategically also requires certain attitudes.

In an interesting article that set out to define the difference between managers and strategists, Hinterhubeer and Popp state two characteristics that make someone a superior strategist. First is the ability to understand the significance of events without being influenced by current opinion, changing attitudes, or one's own prejudices. Second is the ability to make decisions quickly and take the indicated action without being deterred by a perceived danger.

This definition makes more statements about the attitudes required of the good strategist and implementer than it does about the *way* that the strategist achieves the understanding of events. The tenacity element of WIST is vital for the fulfilment of a strategy, but what must the strategic leader consider in order to be an effective strategist?

One of the clearest lists of requirements was made by Stephen Stumpf and Thomas Mullen who identified four elements associated with what they termed 'managerial effectiveness'. These were pictured as the four legs of a table on which sat the business plan. Take away any one leg of the table and it would fall over. The business plan would be lost! The legs that determined effectiveness were:

1. Consistently applying a number of key concepts. Managers must use the concepts of mission, vision, objectives/goals, and strategy as part of their normal pattern of work.

2. The ability to develop skills of thinking and acting strategically.

3. Knowing one's personal style and its impact on other people.

4. Understanding the nature of strategic management processes.

As legs one and three have already been covered in earlier chapters there is more to profit from concentrating on legs two and four.

Leg two

Stumpf and Mullen state that the strategic management skills involve a leader's ability to:

1. *Know the business and its markets*   How the business makes its profits, how the customers have behaved in the past, as well as being able to make predictions on this knowledge.

2. *Manage subunit rivalry*   To this I would add that the strategic thinker needs to be able to anticipate the political consequences of different actions in any situation.

3. *Find and overcome threats*   The leader will need to find and diagnose information and from it to anticipate threats and problems.

Indeed they must continually do this as more information becomes available over time.

4. *Stay on strategy*   This is vital and includes: capitalizing on the organization's strengths; trying to improve its competitive advantage; focusing on the most appropriate markets; and assessing each major planned action against the strategy. Is it in line? Is it appropriate ?

   In this light it is interesting to note that Margaret Thatcher had the reputation of being hard on the strategy and flexible on tactics. This was certainly evident during the year-long miners' strike: it is unlikely that she would have been successful in the long term if her philosophy had been the other way round.

5. *Be an entrepreneurial force*   While not all strategies are connected with entrepreneurialism, the true strategist thinks like an entrepreneur and acts with entrepreneurial zeal whether things are going well or not.

6. *Accommodate adversity*   Starting out on a strategy involves risk; mistakes may be made or parts of the strategy may fail. The leader who has the skills and attitudes to stay on strategy must be prepared to shrug off set-backs and continue energetically.

Leg four

This is all about the getting there, the starting and the execution. Like completing a crossword puzzle, state Stumph and Mullen, there are aspects of discovery. It is possible to start anywhere in a crossword puzzle and you can learn and obtain benefits from previous steps. It is part of the game to change your mind and make corrections. You learn through practice and can get good advice from others.

   The mistake that many managers make in trying to implement a strategy is that they may lose sight of the vision and goals once they become immersed. Furthermore, why should the execution of the strategy proceed logically and systematically? People who have few expectations in this direction will have fewer problems.

The strategic steeplechase

Stumpf and Mullen provide a good list of the requirements made on the strategic thinker. There are, however, two ways in which their analysis could be made harder hitting. The analogy of the business plan supported by the four legs of a table is essentially a static picture rather than a dynamic one. After all, both leadership and strategy implementation imply

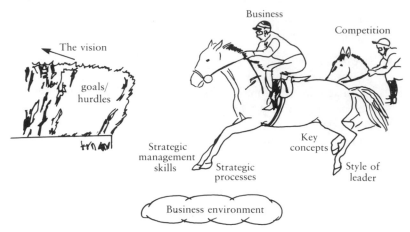

Figure 10.1   The strategic leadership horse and the business steeplechase.

movement. By the same token, as an essentially academic approach the driving desire to achieve the type of perspective that will lead to a winning strategy and then to implement it is not fully felt. The adoption of a different picture to illustrate the same concepts may more fully describe what is required.

Supposing we were to change the static table to a horse in a steeplechase race as in Figure 10.1. The picture now is all about movement. The business plan now is simply the business and is represented by the rider; it must be transported by the horse towards the finishing line. The idea of winning and what it will mean in reward terms for the rider is represented by the finishing line—this is the vision. Between the horse and the finishing line are a number of hurdles that must be jumped. The way in which they are jumped must be planned and will form part of the overall strategy.

Hot on the heels of the horse are other horses and riders whose intent is to beat our horse to the finishing line. They represent the competition; our rider cannot afford to ignore what they are doing and will have carefully weighed up their strengths and weaknesses before the race as well as taking time to monitor them during it. The competition represents part of the business environment, but there are many other elements of the overall business environment that must be considered. How favourable is the overall economic climate? Has the government launched any applicable business incentive schemes? Are the currency exchange rates favourable or not? All of these extraneous economic factors are represented by the track itself. The going may be hard or it may be heavy and no riders worth their salt will embark on the race without first analysing the potential effect of the state of the track on the overall race itself.

But what of the horse? The horse's legs are the equivalent of the table legs; they represent the vital strategic management skills, the use of strategic processes, the need to be aware of the impact of one's own style, and the need to keep a number of key concepts in mind. In order to reach the finishing post, to realize the vision of successfully having moved the business from A to B while staying ahead of the competition, all four legs must be put to work energetically. The strategic leader will do this while also keeping all the other variables in this race firmly in mind.

The analogy of the strategic horse-race lends itself to an exploration of some of the other main adjectives that apply to the leader who starts to think strategically. In describing the move from leadership to strategic thinking, Warren Bennis describes a process that involves developing a perspective of the situation. A good perspective, he states, will lead to a point of view which will stimulate the leader to subject it to tests and measures. If it survives the tests, the leader will have the confidence to desire to succeed and this desire, in turn, will drive the leader to master the situation. Once the leader has mastered the situation, real strategic thinking has been achieved and allows the leader full expression through it. The end result of the strategy is the realization of the vision.

The main point about this alternative and very 'right-brained' approach is that the same emotional adjectives apply as much to strategic thinking as they do to leadership itself. The former is the expression of the latter and so the same prerequisites of emotion, desire, creativity, and determination apply.

Summary

But what then of the millennium leader, this sure-footed but lightly stepping individual who knows how to avoid the traps that ensnare frogs and rhinos? How can we summarize what this leader will need to know and do?

This new breed of leader needs to balance a complex range of require-ments as illustrated in Figure 10.2. To remind us of the need to value the best of the past, I have adapted the three-circle concept that John Adair used for his model of leadership but highlighted the extra concepts that need to be incorporated into the millenium leader's range of skills.

The leader must not forget the existing requirements of leadership. The critical necessity of remembering the needs of the task in hand, the needs of the team that must address the task, and the specific needs of the individuals who make up the team, is paramount. This must be coupled with the ability to crystallize visions and empower others through effective self-expression and the demonstration of the values of WIST. This is shown in circle one.

At the same time, however, the millennium leader must not forget that the process must also be managed. The discipline of planning, directing, co-

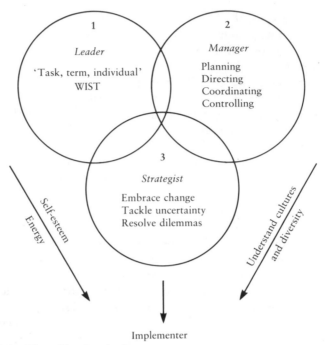

Figure 10.2   The millennium leader.

ordinating, and controlling efforts to achieve successful outcomes is not
something that can be abandoned because fashions of thinking have moved
on. Like the poor, this 'management' requirement is always with us and it
complements the more esoteric needs of the leader to have a clear vision and
to lead the team towards its fulfilment. The tasks implied in achieving the
vision must be made to percolate down to influence people's individual
accountabilities and daily work. This requirement is illustrated in circle two.

Circle three illustrates the third element to be considered. The leader
must be a strategist and must think strategically. Before true strategic
thinking can be born, the leader must come to terms with the concept of
change and must learn to manage it confidently, in effect, to make change
happen. In turn, this necessitates being able to cope with uncertainty and
being able to solve dilemmas through positive, flexible, and creative
thought processes. One such thought process might well be that of coming
to value differences of approach or opinion, rather than seeing them as a
threat, and of being flexible in reacting to the different requirements that
will be made of leaders in the future.

Coping with this array of demands will require a great deal of the
millenium leader. In order to become an implementer (and getting things
done remains the key requirement) the leader must add energy to the
equation and self-esteem to underpin it. Then, with sensitivity to the

culture in which the leader is operating and a fair degree of luck, success should follow.

Put together all three circles and the leader will have the tools to move beyond the helicopter effect. The helicopter is a fine tool as far as it goes, but as you become more senior and the demands on you grow in scope and complexity, you may find the need to move out of the helicopter into the strategic leader's space shuttle. The high orbit that the shuttle achieves and the new perspectives it gives can help you make connections and decisions that elude others. In effect, the shuttle will not only help you to sort out the wood from the trees but also tell you whether or not you are in the right wood!

Your WIFMs from this chapter

- What particular pressures and demands will you face as a result of future changes? What will you do about them?

- How often do you allow yourself to think creatively? What is stopping you?

- Are there any dilemmas or areas of ambiguity affecting your ability to lead? Can you find ways of breaking their hold?

- Could your thinking be boxed in with preconceptions about gender or nationality?

- Can you find the time to think strategically and have you considered what this will require of you?

- Are you a strategic leader, or just a manager?

Taking control of your leadership development

This book has concentrated on the birth and growth of leadership. It has featured the challenging mixture of skills and knowledge required to master that mysterious concept and, more important, to sustain the mastery. It has examined techniques, tools, and theories but in the final analysis it has been about *you*.

No theory or concept is of any value unless it stimulates action and the result of an action is that something will change. The question therefore stands. What are you going to do to answer the challenge of leadership? If being a leader is something that you can choose to do through action and self-discovery, what choices will you make?

There are a number of steps and a clear prerequisite in taking control of your development as a leader. The steps are connected with the process of preparing and undertaking your development while the essential prerequisite is that of having the *will* to do so.

Preparation

There is a school of thought that asserts that leaders invent and grow themselves, that they are self-made and create the sort of person and leader that they wish to become. This is fine at one level but (assuming the will is there) I would contend that there are a number of useful guidelines for aiding an individual's development as a leader.

The first step is that of deciding what it is you want to achieve. Do you really want to be a leader? If so, what sort of leader do you want to become? In what context do you wish to operate? What sort of influence do you wish to exert? Are you truly interested in being a leader and accomplishing things through others, or are you just interested in power?

Having tried to answer this battery of questions, then ask yourself where it is that you want to be in the future and force yourself to put a time-scale on it. This I call 'self-visioning'. The process simply involves asking yourself a number of deceptively simple questions.

Where do you see yourself in career and leadership terms in one year's time? This is easy enough to answer as the time-scale is relatively short and you may be happy to accept that you anticipate no change whatsoever. (Do I hear distant shouts of disagreement from the controller/takers?)

Where do you see yourself in career and leadership terms in five or ten years' time? This is harder. If you really want to be a leader, to be influencing events, to be making change happen, then an answer of 'no change' should be unacceptable. If it is, then the logical next question is: *So, what are you going to do about it?'*

The first step is to take stock.

The SWOT analysis

SWOT is one of the best known and most used tools for strategic planning. It is simple and easy to use and it forces those doing it to look at a business situation from a number of perspectives. It can lead to valuable insights both to the present situation and to what should be done in the future:

S   *Strengths*   What are the organization's strengths? Can they be listed? How can they be augmented?

W   *Weaknesses*   Once again, they need to be listed. What can be done about them? How can their effect be minimized?

O   This refers to the *opportunities* open to the business, both present and future. How can the business capitalize on them?

T   These are the *threats* that face the business. They may stem from the competition, from changes to the business scenario, or from lack of attention to the weaknesses. Once again, what can be done about them?

The SWOT is a powerful tool, it can be brainstormed and therefore encourages teamwork. Its effect is to give a candid overview and challenge those using it to consider future action. The SWOT is even more powerful when you do it on yourself!

The first stage of taking control is to understand yourself and your situation and the understanding will come from this candid stock-take. Take a blank sheet of paper and draw a large cross on it. Then mark it out with the letters SWOT, one letter in each of the boxes made by the cross and start to fill in the boxes. This may not be a comfortable process but total honesty is necessary. Refer back to the various attributes of leadership described in this book—they may give clues to what you perceive to be your strengths and weaknesses.

A number of test questions can then follow:

- How can I match my strengths to the opportunities I perceive?
- Are the threats to me a direct result of my weaknesses?
- Can I convert my weaknesses to strengths? If so, how?
- Can any of the threats be converted to opportunities?

This final question is rather harder to conceptualize but it was driven home hard to me as a result of a resignation.

THE HIDDEN OPPORTUNITY

For several years I had been relying on Chris, my deputy. Chris was an expert at industrial relations and I used to delegate a large amount of the negotiations and day-to-day issues in this field to him. One day, out of the blue, Chris resigned. He had found a position elsewhere and the money was better.

I rushed to see my boss and demanded that we pay Chris a large increase as he was invaluable. To my surprise, the CEO said that we would not prevent him from leaving. I protested energetically but in the end could not counter the argument that my boss presented to me.

It was time for Chris to go. The new position was a good one and represented a positive career step. We would do him no favours by inducing him to hang on with us. At the same time, my boss wanted me to become more involved in the industrial relations side of the business and Chris's leaving would make that much more easy. By the same token, Chris was not strong on human resource planning and his departure gave us the opportunity to recruit someone who had these skills.

The perceived threat therefore, with imagination, could be converted into a number of opportunities.

One opportunity that should always emerge as a result of the SWOT is that of continuing your own personal learning and development in leadership. What then are the mechanisms for this? How can it be done?

Managing your own development

This is where you have a responsibility both to yourself and for yourself. There is one prerequisite, however, before you can effectively learn—*you must unlearn!*

Unlearn? So many opportunities are overlooked because the so-called learner is blinkered by prejudices. Preconceptions of there being only one way to do something or that people always react in a certain way have torpedoed many genuine attempts to learn. The process of unlearning, of deliberately leaving the mind open yet empty of dangerous preconceptions, will speed up development.

Do not confuse this technique with the mistake of ignoring previous experience—that would be foolhardy. However, unlearning will allow you to build on the past more securely while at the same time remaining open to the challenges of new ideas and knowledge. When we are dealing with ourselves it is all too easy to be the hostage of our own pasts and preconceptions about both ourselves and other people. A cynic once said that the process of thinking was simply that of rearranging our prejudices. How true, for some!

A number of ways of managing your own development exist. They can be focused into three distinct challenges:

- Managing your contacts

- Selecting the medium

- Testing your progress

Managing your contacts

Much has been said and written about the value of networking. Effective managers, we are told, work through networks of contacts and make note of people whom it is useful to know. The knowledge may be used in order to pursue potential sales opportunities, to mark those who may be of use when next you place yourself on the job market, or simply to note those people who may possess information that may be useful to you in the future. Effective managers keep a record of the names on their networks and update the lists regularly. But how can networking be of use in the managing of your own leadership development?

Effective leaders, as part of their management function, will probably keep a record of their networks but, in addition, will keep a lookout for possible mentors and models. The responsibility of leaders to develop other leaders was explored in Chapter 7. The responsibility, however, works both ways. Consequently, if being a mentor is a responsibility, then so is the job of finding one. Most top leaders have not been ashamed to have advisors who act in a mentoring role. Therefore, the responsibility to find someone who can give candid and impartial advice is an important one. If the organization does not offer a mentor, look for one. The mentor need not be from within the organization and most people who are asked to fulfil this role are flattered.

Finding a model of leadership is a different task. The mentor and the model need not be the same person and the model need not even know that he or she has been chosen for this role. The model of leadership is an individual whom you admire; you like the way that they lead and you may think that they display particular talents in handling situations.

Examine the model's style carefully. What is it about them that makes them good and what is it about the way that they handle leadership situations that is so effective? Can you pin it down or quantify it? Can you repackage what is good about them so that you can use those behaviours or techniques yourself? One word of caution here. You can never totally model yourself on another person as leaders are, by definition, individuals. You should also check that other people consider your model to be a good leader—if they do not, think again!

A method of leadership development that can be particularly effective and which builds on the model theme, is that of the *masterclass*. This is a forum where would-be leaders are given the opportunity of questioning an acknowledged leader on various aspects of that leader's role and of asking exactly *why* various courses of action had been taken by that leader.

This type of development is based on the assumption that hearing about it from the horse's mouth is of more value than umpteen hours of training or video. Many agree, just as most aspiring violinists would trade many hours of listening to recordings for just one hour in the company of Yehudi Menuhin, Nigel Kennedy, or Stefan Grapelli. In the same way, should most aspiring leaders value this direct contact with an acknowledged 'master'.

Selecting the medium

Leadership can be taught. If leadership is what leaders do then the organized practice that training involves should increase the rate of learning. Although there is no substitute for the experience of actually being a leader, a good training course can so package the necessary range of experiences and self-knowledge that leaders require to prepare people in advance to a greater degree than many would think possible.

It could well be argued that the negative impact of poor leadership is so great that no leader should be let loose on unsuspecting followers without having completed a training course. The question remains then as to what is the right sort of leadership course for you.

A large range of courses exists. Courses vary from the introspective to the rugged and deliver self-knowledge of leadership experience through a variety of means. In the end it is up to you to choose the programme that seems most right for you. A few guidelines, however, exist.

A programme that is all theory will probably be boring, so avoid them. By the same token, a programme that simply concentrates on activities is unlikely to make the vital links to the workplace that are so necessary for proper development. On the other hand, a programme that simply goes in for introspection and self-analysis will be too self-indulgent for many. The answer is to select a programme that deliberately tries to mix theory with practice and which puts stress on skilfully delivered individual feedback. If you are uncertain about whether a programme will deliver this for you, telephone the programme director and quiz him or her about it.

At present a debate is raging over the question of outdoor development. Several programmes are totally based outdoors and subject participants to a variety of physically testing tasks (or ordeals). The question is—what do they teach people about leadership?

For a start it is necessary to separate leadership development from character-building. They are not necessarily the same thing. Furthermore, while it may be testing and enjoyable for some to climb rock faces or dive into freezing waters, it is purgatory for others, and failure to perform in these gung ho activities does not mean that you cannot lead people in the normal work environment, although failure at the time can be extremely humiliating and erode self-confidence.

There have been isolated incidents of people dying or being injured on these types of programmes but, paradoxically, that is not the main issue. A leadership programme is only as good as the quality of its facilitation, the way that those running it can develop themes, give sensitive feedback, and make positive connections between what is going on in the programme and in the workplace. Unfortunately, many of those involved in outdoor programmes do not have relevant commercial experience, and this will inevitably detract from the quality of the learning.

Leadership training courses can use the outdoors to provide leadership experiences, but the most effective tasks are those which are mentally or interpersonally demanding rather than physically challenging. They can be run outdoors and provide a stimulating change from the lecture room, but the quality of the learning will be dependent on the quality of the facilitation and the tutor's ability to make direct linkages to the workplace, not on the number of mountains climbed. So, if outdoor development appears attractive (and it can have huge value) investigate the quality of the organization providing it, especially the experience of its facilitators and their ability to make links to the business environment. The best programmes will probably combine lecture room and practical interpersonal experience with some exercises that may take place outdoors to reinforce the lessons learnt. It is not necessary to undergo physical privations to learn leadership. In fact, a fresh mind that comes from having slept well in a comfortable bed is more likely to assist learning than the exhaustion born of privation, discomfort, and even humiliation.

While outdoor development can be a very powerful tool in team-building, think carefully about its applicability for you in your personal *leadership* development.

Testing your progress

The act of developing yourself as a leader is a journey of exploration that hopefully will end in discovery—discovery of your ability to lead, of the leader within you. This journey of exploration may not always be simple or easy, and you will certainly need to check your progress.

Morris West speaks about journeys of exploration in *The Shoes of the Fisherman*. Although the context is different, what he has to say is very relevant to this journey:

> An exploration is a very special kind of journey. You do not make it like a trip from Rome to Paris. You must never demand to arrive on time and with all your baggage intact. You walk slowly with open eyes and with open minds. When the mountains are too high to climb you march around them and try to measure them from the lowlands. When the jungle is too thick you have to cut your way through it, and not resent too much the labour or the frustration.

So how can progress in this journey of exploration be measured?

The act of seeking feedback from others is important, but not possible in all situations. How then can you conduct a self-audit on your development? The following 'audit plan' may be useful:

1. *Awareness*   Am I aware that there may be new attitudes or behaviours demanded of me and that I may need to change?

2. *Integration*   How can I integrate these new demands into my approach? What is required of me to do so?

3. *Examination*   How is it going? Is it working for me or do I need to do more (or less) in some respects?

4. *Emphasis*   If the new behaviours or attitudes are working for me and are making a difference can I then emphasize them by doing them more frequently and even better as my experience grows?

A couple of other pragmatic tests of your progress complement this audit. First of all, leaders express themselves well and clearly. Often the clarity of their expression can transform a situation, motivating or even inspiring others. How well are you expressing yourself? Plato summed up the need for clarity and its impact when he talked about the *dialectic*. This was a process of discussion which could sort out issues via rational argument and intellectual eagerness, thereby liberating all involved.

Plato believed that the dialectic was a great energizer: 'When the eye of the mind gets really bogged down in a mass of ignorance, the dialectic gently pulls it out and leads it up.'

Even more pragmatic is the fundamental need to be a leader and a manager. One of my favourite cartoons depicts two down-and-outs in a bar. One is saying: 'I spent so much time reading books on leadership and excellence that I forgot to do any work'. Situations need individual effort and management. Lord Weinstock, when asked the reason behind certain of his acquisitions is said to have replied, 'I bought English Electric because they couldn't manage money. I bought AEI because they couldn't manage *anything*!'

All of these tests and measures can work but none of them will be of any use unless the *will to lead* and the *will to learn to lead* exist.

The will to lead

The will cannot be taught, only you can develop it. In order to discover the leader in you, you must *want* to do so. The lion, the tin man, and the scarecrow all wanted to be different even if they thought it was impossible. The level of aspiration may be different for different people in order to be realistic, after all not everybody can be prime minister (thank goodness!), Sir John Harvey-Jones, Richard Branson, Anita Roddick, Sir Richard Greenbury, or Sir Allen Sheppard. But we can all aspire to be better leaders at whatever levels it is that we have personal impact.

In becoming better leaders we are more likely to 'realize ourselves' and to lead fuller lives but, even more important, we are more likely to contribute to the well being of our organizations and the well-being of the people in them.

How do we deal with the will? It is not easy to do so in writing and the final impetus must come from the individual. But there are stories and examples that can energize the will. The following three have exerted powerful influence both in past and modern times.

There is the biblical parable of the talents. In this famous parable the owner of a business gives varying amounts of money to different servants and then asks them to account for it when he returns from a journey. Some invest the money or put it to good use in varying ways to show a return. One servant, however, has simply buried his money in the ground and can show no return. This is the servant who incurs the master's wrath. The great sin was to have been given talents (even if small ones) *and not to have used them!* The talents may have been given to an individual, but are doubly wasted when used to benefit neither that person *nor other people!*

Then there is the true story of Captain Mallory who set out to climb Mount Everest in the pre-war years. Shortly before the ascent he was interviewed by a BBC journalist. The conversation ran something like this:

'Captain Mallory, why do you want to climb Mount Everest?'

Then came the famous reply:

'Because it's there!'

'But Everest is the highest mountain in the world, aren't there great dangers in making the ascent?'

'The greatest dangers lie in *not* making the ascent.'

Mallory went on to attempt the ascent and perished in doing so. After the expedition had returned to Britain several members of the expedition and other mountaineers met for a dinner to honour Mallory's memory. It was an emotional occasion because Mallory had been much loved both as a man and as a leader. A large picture of Everest had been placed on a wall and during the evening a member of the expedition turned and addressed the picture. 'Everest,' he said, 'you have beaten us this time but I promise you that one day we will conquer you. The reason is simple. You cannot grow, but we can!'

The same attitude of refusing to accept discouragement and of proceeding despite set-backs can be seen in the life of Gladys Aylward who, on failing to find a sponsor, travelled to China on money she had laboriously saved up in 'domestic service'. Once there she became involved in prison reform, influenced Mandarins, and led the now famous march of the homeless children to escape the fighting during the war between China and Japan.

The final exhortation comes from a modern film. It is not explicitly about leadership but contains a haunting example of it. In the film *Dead Poets Society*, the schoolmaster, played by Robin Williams, exhorts the boys to *Carpe diem*—to seize the day!

He takes them to look at the fading photographs of previous generations of boys from that school. 'Look at them,' he urges, 'underneath the different fashions they are just like you. There is only one big difference—they are no longer alive and you are. So what is their message to you across the years? It's *carpe diem, carpe diem*!'

Seize the day.

Conclusion—the need for leadership

The effects of leadership are all around us. These effects can, of course, be good or bad and by and large, it is bad leadership, no leadership, or effective leadership applied by bad people that has made this world the dark place that it so often seems. This darkness may be the result of political actions and manifest itself in famine, poverty, or conflict, but this darkness may also exist for countless thousands in their places of work.

However, there is an overwhelming case for optimism. Let us assume that most people have good intentions and that those good intentions, when exercised by leaders wherever they are and at whatever level, can bring about change. Those leaders can help everybody see what needs to be seen and can stimulate action for progress and improvement.

This can happen at a high level, as in the case of Norwegian diplomats' engineering the signing of a recognition document between Israel and the PLO. It can also happen in the thousands of unsung cases where ordinary men and women, through their efforts to be better leaders, bosses, managers, or whatever word you want to use for it, have made a difference not only to the profitability of their organizations but also to the values and working lives of their colleagues within them.

The world may sometimes seem a dark place; in reality it is not, as the major part of most people's work and lives is spent in striving to better the lot of this planet and its inhabitants. The right sort of leader, therefore, is like a light-bearer. One small light may dispel a small area of darkness, but put thousands of small lights together and even the darkest places will shine.

References

J. Adair (1983) *Effective Leadership*. Gower Publishing Company Ltd: London.

D. Barry (1991) 'Managing the Bossless Team: Lessons in Distributed Leadership', *Organizational Dynamics*, summer, vol. 20.

R. Meredith Belbin (1981) *Management Teams*. Butterworth-Heinemann: Oxford.

R. Meredith Belbin, 'Solo Leader: Antithesis in Style and Structure', published in *Frontiers of Leadership* (1992) eds M. Syrett and C. Hogg. Blackwell Publishers: Oxford.

S. L. Benn (1974) 'The Measurement of Psychological Androgny', *Journal of Counselling and Clinical Psychology*.

W. Bennis (1989) *On Becoming a Leader*. Addison-Wesley Publishing Company: USA.

K. H. Blanchard and S. Johnson (1982) *The One-Minute Manager*. William Morrow: USA.

D. Drennan (1992) *Transforming Company Culture*. McGraw-Hill Book Company: Maidenhead.

R. Eales-Whyte (1992) *The Power of Persuasion*. Kogan Page: London.

C. Emmins, 'The Lessons of Motivation', published in *Managing 1992. The Competitive Business*, ed. R. Heller. Sterling Publishing Group PLC: London.

C. Hampden Turner (1990) *Charting the Corporate Mind*. The Free Press (a division of Macmillan Inc. Basil Blackford): Oxford.

R. Harrison (1991) *Humanising Change. Matching Interventions to Organisational Realities*. Copyright Harrison Associates 1991.

C. Handy (1989) *The Age of Unreason*. Business Books Ltd: London.

N. Hermann (1988) *The Creative Brain*. Brain Books: NC, USA.

P. Herriot (1992) *The Career Management Challenge*. Sage Publications Ltd: London.

P. Hersey and K. H. Blanchard (1977) *Management of Organisational Behaviour: Utilising Human Resources*, 3rd edn. Prentice-Hall: Englewood Cliffs, N.J.

H. H. Hinterbubeer and W. Popp (1992) 'Are you a strategist or just a manager?', *Harvard Business Review*. Harvard University Press: Harvard, MA., Jan–Feb.

L. Iacocca with W. Novak (1984) *Iacocca: an Autobiography*. Bantam Books: USA and Canada.

R. M. Kanter (1989) *When Giants Learn to Dance*. Simon & Schuster: New York.

R. E. Kelly (1988) 'In Praise of Followers', *Harvard Business Review*. Harvard University Press: Harvard, USA.

M. Kets de Vries (1989) *Prisoners of Leadership*. John Wiley & Sons: USA.

J. Kotter (1988) *The Leadership Factor*. Free Press: New York.

A. H. Maslow (1948) 'A Theory of Human Needs', *Psychological Review*.

J. Nichols (1988) 'Meta Leadership in Organisations. Applying Burn's Political Concept of Transforming Leadership'. *Leader and Organizational Development Journal*, no. 9 (2).

A. Pease (1981) *Body Language: How to read others' thoughts by their gestures*. Sheldon Press: London

T. J. Peters and R. H. Waterman, Jnr (1982) *In Search of Excellence*. Harper & Row: New York.

L. W. Porter and E. E. Lawler (1968) *Managing Organisational Behaviour*. Richard D. Irwin: Homewood, Ill.

J. B. Rosner (1990) 'Ways Women Lead', *Harvard Business Review*. Harvard University Press: Harvard, MA.

P. M. Senge (1990) *The Fifth Discipline*. Doubleday: USA.

B. Smith and G. Morphey (1994) 'Tough Challenges. How Big a Learning Gap?' *Journal of Management Development*. UK.

R. Stewart (1982) *Choices for the Manager*. McGraw-Hill Book Company: Maidenhead.

S. Stumph and T. P. Mullen (1991) 'Strategic Leadership, Style and Process', *Journal of Management Development* (10). MCB University Press.

R. Tannenbaum and W. H. Schmidt (1958) 'How to Choose a Leadership Pattern', *Harvard Business Review*, 36 (2). Harvard University Press: Harvard, MA.

B. W. Tuchman, (1965) 'Developmental Sequence in Small Groups', *Psychological Bulletin*, 63.

M. West (1963) *The Shoes of the Fisherman*. William Heinemann Ltd. and Pan Books: London.

J. Zenger, E. Musselwhite, K. Hudson and C. Perrion (1991) 'Leadership in a Team Environment', *Training and Development*. USA.

Index